Islamic State of Iraq and Syria (ISIS) Reconciliation, Democracy and Terror

ISLAMIC STATE OF IRAQ AND SYRIA(ISIS)

RECONCILIATION, DEMOCRACY AND TERROR

Col. S.C.Dhiman (Retd.)

NEHA PUBLISHERS & DISTRIBUTORS

DELHI

Publisher
NEHA PUBLISHERS & DISTRIBUTORS
4832/24,Prahlad Lane,S-207 Ansari
Road, Daryaganj, Delhi-110002
Ph.: 43570976, 23278261
Email: nehapubdistributors@gmail.com

Edition: 2015

ISBN: 978-93-80318-67-7

Laser Typesetting
JEE-VEE Graphics, Delhi

Price: 325/-

Printed

Vikas Computers, Delhi

Preface

The ISIS was preceded by the Islamic State of Iraq (ISI), that was established during October 2006, and comprised of various insurgent groups, most significantly the original Al Qaeda Organization in the Land of the Two Rivers (AQI) organization, al-Qaeda in Mesopotami - led by Abu Musab al-Zarqawi, the Mujahedeen Shura Council in Iraq, and Jund al-Sahhaba (Soldiers of the Prophet's Companions), which was integrated into the ISI. ISIS members' allegiance was given to the ISI commander and not al-Qaeda central command. The organisation known as the ISIS was formed during April 2013 and has evolved in one of the main jihadist groups fighting government forces in Syria and Iraq. ISIS regards Baquba, Iraq, as its headquarters with its allegiance to Abu Omar al-Baghdadi as the group's emir. Baghdadi's real name is Hamed Dawood Mohammed Khalil al-Zawi.

ISIS grew significantly as an organization owing to its participation in the Syrian Civil War and the strength of its leader, Abu Bakr al-Baghdadi. Economic and political discrimination against Arab Iraqi Sunnis since the fall of the secular Saddam Hussein also helped it to gain support. At the height of the 2003–2011 Iraq War, its forerunners enjoyed a significant presence in the Iraqi governorates of Al Anbar, Nineveh, Kirkuk, most of Salah ad Din, parts of Babil, Diyala and Baghdad, and claimed Baqubah as a capital city. In the ongoing Syrian Civil War, ISIS has a large presence in the Syrian governorates of Ar-Raqqah, Idlib and Aleppo.

This book maintains that the source of the terror that we condemn is definitely not from a divine religion, and that there is no room for terrorism.

—Editor

Contents

1

Introduction

The Islamic State (IS) also known as the Islamic State of Iraq and the Levant (ISIL) and the Islamic State of Iraq and Syria (ISIS) is a jihadist group, widely regarded as a terrorist organisation. In its self-proclaimed status as a caliphate, it claims religious authority over all Muslims across the world and aspires to bring much of the Muslim-inhabited regions of the world under its direct political control, beginning with territory in the Levant region, which includes Jordan, Israel, Palestine, Lebanon, Cyprus, and an area in southern Turkey that includes Hatay. The group has been officially designated as a foreign terrorist organization by the United States, the United Kingdom, Australia, Canada, Indonesia, and Saudi Arabia, and has been widely described as a terrorist group by Western and Middle Eastern media sources.

The group, in its original form, was composed of and supported by a variety of Sunni Arab terrorist insurgent groups, including its predecessor organizations, Al-Qaeda in Iraq (AQI) (2003–2006), Mujahideen Shura Council (2006–2006) and the Islamic State of Iraq (ISI) (2006–2013), other insurgent groups such as Jeish al-Taiifa al-Mansoura, Jaysh al-Fatiheen, Jund al-Sahaba and Katbiyan Ansar Al-Tawhid wal Sunnah, and a number of Iraqi tribes that profess Sunni Islam.

ISIS grew significantly as an organization owing to its participation in the Syrian Civil War and the strength of its leader, Abu Bakr al-Baghdadi. Economic and political discrimination against Arab Iraqi Sunnis since the fall of the secular Saddam Hussein also helped it to gain support. At the height of the 2003–

2011 Iraq War, its forerunners enjoyed a significant presence in the Iraqi governorates of Al Anbar, Nineveh, Kirkuk, most of Salah ad Din, parts of Babil, Diyala and Baghdad, and claimed Baqubah as a capital city. In the ongoing Syrian Civil War, ISIS has a large presence in the Syrian governorates of Ar-Raqqah, Idlib and Aleppo.

ISIS is known for its extreme and brutally harsh interpretation of the Islamic faith and sharia law and has a record of horrifying violence, which is directed at Shia Muslims, indigenous Assyrian/ Chaldean/Syriac Christians and Armenian Christians, Yazidis, Druze, Shabakis and Mandeans in particular. It has at least 4,000 fighters in its ranks in Iraq who, in addition to attacks on government and military targets, have claimed responsibility for attacks that have killed thousands of civilians. ISIS had close links with al-Qaeda until 2014, but in February of that year, after an eight-month power struggle, al-Qaeda cut all ties with the group, reportedly for its brutality and "notorious intractability".

ISIS's original aim was to establish a caliphate in the Sunni-majority regions of Iraq. Following its involvement in the Syrian Civil War, this expanded to include controlling Sunni-majority areas of Syria. A caliphate was proclaimed on 29 June 2014, Abu Bakr al-Baghdadi—now known as Amir al-Mu'minin Caliph Ibrahim—was named as its caliph, and the group was renamed the Islamic State.

NAME AND NAME CHANGES

The group has had a number of different names since its formation in early 2004 as *Jamâ៴at al-Taw per cent៴îd wa-al-Jihâd,* "The Organization of Monotheism and Jihad" (JTJ). These names are underscored in the following paragraphs.

In October 2004, the group's leader Abu Musab al-Zarqawi swore loyalty to Osama bin Laden and changed the name of the group to *Tan៴îm Qâ៴idat al-Jihâd fî Bilâd al-Râfidayn,* "The Organization of Jihad's Base in the Country of the Two Rivers", more commonly known as "Al-Qaeda in Iraq" (AQI). Although the group has never called itself "Al-Qaeda in Iraq", this name has frequently been used to describe it through its various incarnations. In January 2006, AQI merged with several smaller Iraqi insurgent groups under an umbrella organization called the "Mujahideen Shura Council". This was little more than a media exercise and an attempt to give the group a more Iraqi flavour and perhaps to distance al-Qaeda from some of al-Zarqawi's tactical errors, notably the 2005 bombings by AQI of three hotels in Amman. Al-Zarqawi was killed in June 2006, after which the group's direction shifted again.

On 12 October 2006, the Mujahideen Shura Council joined four more insurgent factions and the representatives of a number of Iraqi Arab tribes, and together they swore the traditional Arab oath of allegiance known as *$ɤilf al-Mumɤayyabîn* ("Oath of the Scented Ones"). During the ceremony, the participants swore to free Iraq's Sunnis from what they described as Shia and foreign oppression, and to further the name of Allah and restore Islam to glory.

On 13 October 2006, the establishment of the *Dawlat al-ɤIraq al-Islâmîyah,* "Islamic State of Iraq" (ISI) was announced. A cabinet was formed and Abu Abdullah al-Rashid al-Baghdadi became ISI's figurehead emir, with the real power residing with the Egyptian Abu Ayyub al-Masri. The declaration was met with hostile criticism, not only from ISI's jihadist rivals in Iraq, but from leading jihadist ideologues outside the country. Al-Baghdadi and al-Masri were both killed in a US–Iraqi operation in April 2010. The next leader of the ISI was Abu Bakr al-Baghdadi, the current leader of ISIS.

On 9 April 2013, having expanded into Syria, the group adopted the name "Islamic State of Iraq and the Levant", also known as "Islamic State of Iraq and al-Sham". The name is abbreviated as ISIS or alternately ISIL. The final "S" in the acronym ISIS stems from the Arabic word *Shâm* (or *Shaam*), which in the context of global jihad refers to the Levant or Greater Syria. ISIS was also known as *al-Dawlah* ("the State"), or *al-Dawlah al-Islâmîyah* ("the Islamic State"). These are short-forms of the Arabic name for the "Islamic State of Iraq and al-Sham"; it is similar to calling "the United States of America" "the States".

ISIS's detractors, particularly in Syria, refer to the group as "*Da'ish*" or "*Daesh*",, a term that is based on an acronym formed from the letters of the name in Arabic, *al-Dawla al-Islamiya fi Iraq wa al-Sham*. The group considers the term derogatory and reportedly uses flogging as a punishment for people who use the acronym in ISIS-controlled areas.

On 14 May 2014, the United States Department of State announced its decision to use "Islamic State of Iraq and the Levant" (ISIL) as the group's primary name. The debate over which acronym should be used to designate the group, ISIL or ISIS, has been discussed by several commentators. Ishaan Tharoor from *The Washington Post* concluded: "In the larger battlefield of copy style controversies, the distinction between ISIS or ISIL is not so great."

On 29 June 2014, the establishment of a new caliphate was announced, with Abu Bakr al-Baghdadi named as its caliph, and the group formally changed its name to the "Islamic State".

Ideology and Beliefs

ISIS is an extremist group that follows al-Qaeda's hard-line ideology and adheres to global jihadist principles. Like al-Qaeda and many other modern-day jihadist groups, ISIS emerged from the ideology of the Muslim Brotherhood, the world's first Islamist group dating back to the late 1920s in Egypt. ISIS follows an extreme anti-Western interpretation of Islam, promotes religious violence and regards those who do not agree with its interpretations as infidels and apostates. Concurrently, ISIS (now IS) aims to establish a Salafist-orientated Islamist state in Iraq, Syria and other parts of the Levant.

ISIS's ideology originates in the branch of modern Islam that aims to return to the early days of Islam, rejecting later "innovations" in the religion which it believes corrupt its original spirit. It condemns later caliphates and the Ottoman empire for deviating from what it calls pure Islam and hence has been attempting to establish its own caliphate. However, there are some Sunni commentators, Zaid Hamid, for example, and even Salafi and jihadi muftis such as Adnan al-Aroor and Abu Basir al-Tartusi, who say that ISIS and related terrorist groups are not Sunnis at all, but Kharijite heretics serving an imperial anti-Islamic agenda.

Salafists such as ISIS believe that only a legitimate authority can undertake the leadership of jihad, and that the first priority over other areas of combat, such as fighting against non-Muslim countries, is the purification of Islamic society. For example, when it comes to the Israeli–Palestinian conflict, since ISIS regards the Palestinian Sunni group Hamas as apostates who have no legitimate authority to lead jihad, it regards fighting Hamas as the first step towards confrontation with Israel.

Goals

From its beginnings the establishment of a pure Islamic state has been one of the group's main goals. According to journalist Sarah Birke, one of the "significant differences" between Al-Nusra Front and ISIS is that ISIS "tends to be more focused on establishing its own rule on conquered territory". While both groups share the ambition to build an Islamic state, ISIS is "far more ruthless... carrying out sectarian attacks and imposing sharia law immediately". ISIS finally achieved its goal on 29 June 2014, when it removed "Iraq and the Levant" from its name, began to refer to itself as the Islamic State, and declared the territory which it occupied in Iraq and Syria a new caliphate.

In mid-2014, the group released a video entitled "The End of Sykes–Picot" featuring an English-speaking Chilean national named Abu Safiyya. The video announced the group's intention to eliminate all modern borders between Islamic Middle Eastern countries; this was a reference to the borders set by the Sykes–Picot Agreement during World War I.

TERRITORIAL CLAIMS

On 13 October 2006, the group announced the establishment of the Islamic State of Iraq, which claimed authority over the Iraqi governorates of Baghdad, Anbar, Diyala, Kirkuk, Salah al-Din, Nineveh, and parts of Babil. Following the 2013 expansion of the group into Syria and the announcement of the Islamic State of Iraq and the Levant, the number of wilayah—provinces—which it claimed increased to 16. In addition to the seven Iraqi wilayah, the Syrian divisions, largely lying along existing provincial boundaries, are Al Barakah, Al Kheir, Ar-Raqqah, Al Badiya, Halab, Idlib, Hama, Damascus and the Coast.

In Syria, ISIS's seat of power is in Ar-Raqqah Governorate. Top ISIS leaders, including Abu Bakr al-Baghdadi, are known to have visited its provincial capital, Ar-Raqqah.

Analysis

After significant setbacks for the group during the latter stages of the coalition forces' presence in Iraq, by late 2012 it was thought to have renewed its strength and more than doubled the number of its members to about 2,500, and since its formation in April 2013, ISIS has grown rapidly in strength and influence in Iraq and Syria. Analysts have underlined the deliberate inflammation of sectarian conflict between Iraqi Shias and Sunnis during the Iraq War by various Sunni and Shiite actors as the root cause of ISIS's rise. The post-invasion policies of the international coalition forces have also been cited as a factor, with Fanar Haddad, a research fellow at the National University of Singapore's Middle East Institute, blaming the coalition forces during the Iraq War for "enshrining identity politics as the key marker of Iraqi politics". ISIS's violence is directed particularly against Shia Muslims and indigenous Assyrian/Chaldean/Syriac Christians and Armenian Christians. In June 2014, *The Economist* reported that "ISIS may have up to 6,000 fighters in Iraq and 3,000–5,000 in Syria, including perhaps 3,000 foreigners; nearly a thousand are reported to hail from Chechnya and perhaps 500 or so more from France, Britain and elsewhere in Europe". Chechen fighter Abu Omar al-Shishani, for example, was made commander of the northern sector of ISIS in Syria in 2013.

By 2014, ISIS was increasingly being viewed as a militia rather than a terrorist group. As major Iraqi cities fell to al-Baghdadi's cohorts in June, Jessica Lewis, an expert on ISIS at the Institute for the Study of War, described ISIS as "not a terrorism problem anymore", but rather "an army on the move in Iraq and Syria, and they are taking terrain. They have shadow governments in and around Baghdad, and they have an aspirational goal to govern. I don't know whether they want to control Baghdad, or if they want to destroy the functions of the Iraqi state, but either way the outcome will be disastrous for Iraq." Lewis, who was a US Army intelligence officer in Iraq and Afghanistan, has called ISIS "an advanced military leadership". She said, "They have incredible command and control and they have a sophisticated reporting mechanism from the field that can relay tactics and directives up and down the line.

They are well-financed, and they have big sources of manpower, not just the foreign fighters, but also prisoner escapees." ISIS's annual reports reveal a metrics-driven military command, according to the Institute for the Study of War, which is "a strong indication of a unified, coherent leadership structure that commands from the top down". Middle East Forum's Aymenn Jawad Al-Tamimi said, "They are highly skilled in urban guerrilla warfare while the new Iraqi Army simply lacks tactical competence." Seasoned observers point to systemic corruption within the Iraq Army, it being little more than a system of patronage, and have attributed to this its spectacular collapse as ISIS and its allies took over large swaths of Iraq in June 2014.

Hillary Clinton stated: "The failure to help build up a credible fighting force of the people who were the originators of the protests against Assad—there were Islamists, there were secularists, there was everything in the middle—the failure to do that left a big vacuum, which the jihadists have now filled."

During the Iraq War, the US Armed Forces had never faced an organized militant force as effective. Douglas Ollivant, a former Army Cavalry officer who later handled Iraq for the White House National Security Council, said, "They were great terrorists. They made great car bombs. But they were lousy line infantry, and if you got them in a firefight, they'd die. They have now repaired that deficiency." Like other analysts, Ollivant credits the civil war in Syria for their striking improvement in battlefield ability since the Iraq War: "You fight Hizballah for a couple of years, and you either die or you get a lot better. And these guys just got a lot better." Another major weapon in ISIS's tactical armoury is control of rivers, dams, and water installations.

ISIS runs a soft-power programme, which includes social services, religious lectures and *da'wah*—proselytizing—to local populations. It also performs civil tasks such as repairing roads and maintaining the electricity supply.

PROPAGANDA AND SOCIAL MEDIA

The group is also known for its effective use of propaganda. In November 2006, shortly after the creation of the Islamic State of Iraq, the group established the al-Furqan Institute for Media Production, which produced CDs, DVDs, posters, pamphlets, and web-related propaganda products. ISIS's main media outlet is the I'tisaam Media Foundation, which was formed in March 2013 and distributes through the Global Islamic Media Front (GIMF). In 2014, ISIS established the Al Hayat Media Center, which targets a Western audience and produces material in English, German, Russian and French. In 2014 it also launched the Ajnad Media Foundation, which releases jihadist audio chants.

ISIS's use of social media has been described by one expert as "probably more sophisticated than [that of] most US companies". It regularly takes advantage of social media, particularly Twitter, to distribute its message by organizing hashtag campaigns, encouraging Tweets on popular hashtags, and utilizing software applications that enable ISIS propaganda to be distributed to its supporters' accounts. Another comment is that "ISIS puts more emphasis on social media than other jihadi groups.... They have a very coordinated social media presence." Although ISIS's social media feeds on Twitter are regularly shut down, it frequently recreates them, maintaining a strong online presence. The group has attempted to branch out into alternate social media sites, such as Quitter, Friendica and Diaspora; Quitter and Friendica, however, almost immediately removed ISIS's presence from their sites.

Finances

A study of 200 documents—personal letters, expense reports and membership rosters—captured from Al-Qaeda in Iraq and the Islamic State of Iraq was carried out by the RAND Corporation in 2014. It found that from 2005 until 2010, outside donations amounted to only 5 per cent of the group's operating budgets, with the rest being raised within Iraq. In the time-period studied, cells were required to send up to 20 per cent of the income generated from kidnapping, extortion rackets and other activities to the next level of the group's leadership. Higher-ranking commanders would then redistribute the funds to provincial or local cells that were in difficulties or needed money to conduct attacks. The records show that the Islamic State of Iraq was dependent on members from Mosul for cash, which the leadership used to provide additional funds to struggling militants in Diyala, Salahuddin and Baghdad. In mid-2014, Iraqi intelligence extracted information from an ISIS operative which revealed that the organization had assets worth US$2 billion, making it the richest jihadist group in the world. About three quarters of this sum is said to be represented by assets seized after the group captured Mosul in June 2014; this includes possibly up to US$429 million looted from Mosul's central bank, along with additional millions and a large quantity of gold bullion stolen from a number of other banks in Mosul. However, doubt was later cast on whether ISIS was able to retrieve anywhere near that sum from the central bank, and even on whether the bank robberies had actually occurred.

ISIS has routinely practised extortion, by demanding money from truck drivers and threatening to blow up businesses, for example. Robbing banks and gold shops has been another source of income. The group is widely reported as receiving funding from private donors in the Gulf states, and both Iran and Iraqi Prime Minister Nouri al-Maliki have accused Saudi Arabia and Qatar of funding ISIS, although there is reportedly no evidence that this is the case.

The group is also believed to receive considerable funds from its operations in Eastern Syria, where it has commandeered oilfields and engages in smuggling out raw materials and archaeological artifacts. ISIS also generates revenue from producing crude oil and selling electric power in northern Syria. Some of this electricity is reportedly sold back to the Syrian government.

Since 2012, ISIS has produced annual reports giving numerical information on its operations, somewhat in the style of corporate reports, seemingly in a bid to encourage potential donors.

Equipment

ISIS has been able to strengthen its military capability by capturing large quantities of weaponry from both Iraq and Syria.

These weapons seizures have improved the group's capacity to carry out successful subsequent operations and obtain more equipment. Weaponry that ISIS has reportedly captured and employed include SA-7 and Stinger surface-to-air missiles, M79 Osa, HJ-8 and AT-4 Spigot anti-tank weapons, Type 59 field guns and M198 howitzers, Humvees, T-54/55 and T-72 main battle tanks, truck mounted DShK guns, ZU-23-2 anti-aircraft guns, BM-21 Grad multiple rocket launchers and at least one Scud missile.

When ISIS captured Mosul Airport in June 2014, it seized a number of UH-60 Blackhawk helicopters and cargo planes that were stationed there. However, according to Peter Beaumont of *The Guardian*, it seemed unlikely that ISIS would be able to deploy them.

ISIS captured nuclear materials from Mosul University in July 2014. In a letter to UN Secretary-General Ban Ki-moon, Iraq's UN Ambassador Mohamed Ali Alhakim said that the materials had been kept at the university and "can be used in manufacturing weapons of mass destruction". Nuclear experts regarded the threat as insignificant. International Atomic Energy Agency spokeswoman Gill Tudor said that the seized materials were "low grade and would not present a significant safety, security or nuclear proliferation risk".

TIMELINE OF EVENTS

2014 events:

- *3 January:* ISIS proclaimed an Islamic state in Fallujah. After prolonged tensions, the newly formed Army of Mujahedeen, the Free Syrian Army and the Islamic Front launched an offensive against ISIS-held territory in the Syrian provinces of Aleppo and Idlib. A spokesman for the rebels said that rebels had attacked ISIS in up to 80 per cent of all ISIS-held villages in Idlib and 65 per cent of those in Aleppo.
- *4 January:* ISIS claimed responsibility for the car-bomb attack on 2 January that killed four people and wounded dozens in the southern Beirut suburb of Haret Hreik, a Hezbollah bastion.

- By 6 January, Syrian rebels had managed to expel ISIS forces from the city of Ar-Raqqah, ISIS's largest stronghold and capital of Ar-Raqqah province. Several weeks later ISIS took the city back.
- *8 January:* Syrian rebels expelled most ISIS forces from the city of Aleppo. However, ISIS reinforcements from Deir ez-Zor province managed to retake several neighbourhoods of the city of Ar-Raqqah. By mid-January ISIS fighters had retaken the entire city of Ar-Raqqah, while rebels expelled ISIS fighters fully from Aleppo city and the villages west of it.
- *25 January:* ISIS announced the creation of its new Lebanese arm, pledging to fight the Shia militant group Hezbollah and its supporters in Lebanon.
- *29 January:* Turkish aircraft near the border fired on an ISIS convoy inside Aleppo province in Syria, killing 11 ISIS fighters and one ISIS emir.
- *30 January:* ISIS fired on border patrol soldiers in Turkey. The Turkish Army retaliated with Panter howitzers and destroyed the ISIS convoy.
- In late January, it was confirmed that Syrian rebels had assassinated ISIS's second-in-command, Haji Bakr, who was al-Qaeda's military council head and a former military officer in Saddam Hussein's army.
- *3 February:* Al-Qaeda's general command broke off its links with ISIS, reportedly to concentrate the Islamist effort on unseating President Bashar al-Assad.
- By mid-February, Al-Nusra Front had joined the battle in support of rebel forces, and expelled ISIS forces from Deir ez-Zor province in Syria.
- By March, ISIS forces had fully retreated from Syria's Idlib province after battles against the Syrian rebels.
- *4 March:* ISIS retreated from the Aleppo province–Turkey border town of Azaz and nearby villages, choosing instead to consolidate around Ar-Raqqah in anticipation of an escalation of fighting with Al-Nusra.

- *8 March:* During an interview with French television channel France 24, Iraqi Prime Minister Nouri al-Maliki accused Saudi Arabia and Qatar of openly funding ISIS.
- *20 March:* In Niðde city in Turkey, three ethnic Albanian members of ISIS—Benjamin Xu, Çendrim Ramadani and Muhammed Zakiri—opened fire while hijacking a truck which killed one police officer and one gendarmerie officer and wounded five people. Shortly after their arrest, Polis Özel Harekat teams launched a series of operations against ISIS in Ýstanbul. Police found documents and an ISIS flag in one place and two Azerbaijanis were arrested.
- *27 April:* Iraqi military helicopters reportedly attacked and destroyed an ISIS convoy of eight vehicles inside Syria. This may be the first time that Iraqi forces have struck outside their country since the Gulf War.1 May: ISIS carried out a total of seven public executions in the city of Ar-Raqqah, northern Syria. Pictures that emerged from the city show how ISIS had been carrying out public crucifixions in areas under its control. In most of these crucifixions, the victims were shot first and their bodies then displayed, but there were also reports of crucifixions preceding the victims being shot or decapitated. In one case a man was said to have been "crucified alive for eight hours", but there was no indication of whether he died.
- In early June, following its large-scale offensives in Iraq, ISIS was reported to have seized control of most of Mosul, the second most populous city in Iraq, a large part of the surrounding Nineveh province, and the city of Fallujah. ISIS also took control of Tikrit, the administrative center of the Salah ad Din Governorate, with the ultimate goal of capturing Baghdad, the Iraqi capital. ISIS was believed to have only 2,000–3,000 fighters up until the Mosul campaign, but during that campaign it became evident that this number was a gross underestimate.
- Also in June, there were reports that a number of Sunni groups in Iraq that were opposed to the predominantly Shia government had joined ISIS, thus bolstering the group's

numbers. However, the Kurds—who are mostly Sunnis—in the northeast of Iraq were unwilling to be drawn into the conflict, and there were clashes in the area between ISIS and the Kurdish Peshmerga.

- *5 June:* ISIS militants stormed the city of Samarra, Iraq, before being ousted from the city by airstrikes mounted by the Iraqi military.
- *6 June:* ISIS militants carried out multiple attacks in the city of Mosul, Iraq.
- *7 June:* ISIS militants took over the University of Anbar in Ramadi, Iraq and held 1,300 students hostage before being ousted by the Iraqi military.
- *9 June:* Mosul fell to ISIS control. The militants seized control of government offices, the airport and police stations. Militants also looted the Central Bank in Mosul, reportedly absconding with US$429 million. More than 500,000 people fled Mosul to escape ISIS. Mosul is a strategic city as it is at a crossroad between Syria and Iraq, and poses the threat of ISIS seizing control of oil production.
- *11 June:* ISIS seized the Turkish consulate in the Iraqi city of Mosul and kidnapped the head of the diplomatic mission and several staff members. ISIS seized the Iraqi city of Tikrit.
- *12 June:* Human Rights Watch, an international human rights advocacy organization, issued a statement about the growing threat to civilians in Iraq.
- *13 June:* Navi Pillay, UN High Commissioner for Human Rights, expressed alarm at reports that ISIS fighters "have been actively seeking out—and in some cases killing—soldiers, police and others, including civilians, whom they perceive as being associated with the government".
- *15 June:* ISIS militants captured the Iraqi city of Tal Afar in the province of Nineveh. ISIS claimed that 1,700 Iraqi soldiers who had surrendered in the fighting had been executed, and released many images of mass executions via its Twitter feed and various web sites.

- *22 June:* ISIS militants captured two key crossings in Anbar, a day after seizing the border crossing at Al-Qaim, a town in a province which borders Syria. According to analysts, capturing these crossings could aid ISIS in transporting weapons and equipment to different battlefields.
- *24 June:* The Syrian Air Force bombed ISIS positions in Iraq. Iraqi Prime Minister Nouri al-Maliki stated: "There was no coordination involved, but we welcome this action. We welcome any Syrian strike against ISIS because this group targets both Iraq and Syria."
- *25 June:* Al-Nusra Front's branch in the Syrian town of al-Bukamal pledged loyalty to ISIS, thus bringing to a close months of fighting between the two groups.
- *25 June:* In an interview with the BBC Arabic service, Prime Minister Nouri al-Maliki said that Iraq had purchased used Sukhoi fighter jets from Russia and Belarus to battle ISIS militants after delays in the delivery of F-16 fighters purchased from the US. "[If] we had air cover, we would have averted what happened", he said.
- *26 June:* Iraq launched its first counterattack against ISIS's advance with an airborne assault designed to seize back control of Tikrit University.
- *28 June:* The Jerusalem Post reported that the Obama administration had requested US$500 million from the US Congress to use in the training and arming of "moderate" Syrian rebels fighting against the Syrian government, in order to counter the growing threat posed by ISIS in Syria and Iraq.
- *29 June:* ISIS announced the establishment of a new caliphate. Abu Bakr al-Baghdadi was appointed its caliph, and the group formally changed its name to the Islamic State.
- *2 July:* Abu Bakr al-Baghdadi, the self-proclaimed caliph of the new Islamic State, said that Muslims should unite to capture Rome in order to "own the world". He called on Muslims the world over to unite behind him as their leader.

- *3 July:* ISIS captured Syria's largest oilfield from rival Islamist fighters, Al-Nusra Front, who put up no resistance to the attack. Taking control of the al-Omar oilfield gave ISIS access to potentially useful crude oil reserves.
- *17 July:* Syria's Shaer gas field in the Homs Governorate was seized by the Islamic State. According to the Syrian Observatory for Human Rights, at least 90 National Defence Force guards defending the field were killed, as were 21 ISIS fighters. The SOHR later put the death toll from the fighting and executions at 270 soldiers, militiamen and staff, and at least 40 ISIS fighters.
- *19 July:* ISIS claimed responsibility for a suicide bombing which killed 33 people and left more than 50 wounded. The explosion occurred in Baghdad's Kadhimiya district, which is the site of a major Shia shrine.
- *24 July:* ISIS blew up the Mosque and tomb of the Prophet Yunus (Jonah) in Mosul, with no reported casualties. Residents in the area said that ISIS had erased a piece of Iraqi heritage.
- *26 July:* ISIS blew up the Nabi Shiyt (Prophet Seth) shrine in Mosul. Sami al-Massoudi, deputy head of the Shia endowment agency which oversees holy sites, confirmed the destruction and added that ISIS had taken artifacts from the shrine to an unknown location.
- *28 July:* To mark the Muslim holy festival of Eid al-Fitr, which ends the period of Ramadan, ISIS released and circulated a 30-minute video showing graphic scenes of mass executions.
- The UN reported that of the 1,737 fatal casualties of the Iraq conflict during July, 1,186 were civilians.
- *1 August:* The Indonesian BNPT (id) declared ISIS a terrorist organization.
- *2 August:* The Iraqi Army confirmed that 37 loyalist fighters had died during combat with Islamic State militants south of Baghdad and in Mosul. The Patriotic Union of Kurdistan (PUK) claimed that "hundreds" of IS militiamen had died in the action.

- *3 August:* IS fighters occupied the city of Zumar and an oilfield in the north of Iraq, after a battle against Kurdish forces.
- *5 August:* Al Jazeera reported that an IS offensive in the Sinjar area of northern Iraq had forced 30,000–50,000 Yazidis to flee into the mountains fearing they would be killed by the IS. They had been threatened with death if they refused conversion to Islam. A UN representative said that "a humanitarian tragedy is unfolding in Sinjar".
- *6 August:* The Islamic State kidnapped 400 Yazidi women in Sinjar to sell them as sex slaves.
- *7 August:* IS fighters took control of the town of Qaraqosh in the province of Nineveh in northern Iraq, which forced its large Christian population to flee.
- *7 August:* President Obama authorized targeted airstrikes in Iraq against ISIS, along with airdrops of aid. The UK offered the US assistance with surveillance and refuelling, and planned humanitarian airdrops to Iraqi refugees.
- *8 August:* The US asserted that the systematic destruction of the Yazidi people by the Islamic State was genocide. The US military launched indefinite airstrikes targeting Islamic State fighters, equipment and installations, with humanitarian aid support from the UK and France, in order to protect civilians in northern Iraq. The Islamic State had advanced to within 30 km of Erbil in northern Iraq. The UK is also considering joining the US in airstrikes.
- *10 August:* France's Foreign Minister Laurent Fabius said that Iraq's Kurds must be equipped to fight against ISIS and indicated that France would consider providing arms aid "in liaison with the Europeans". Islamic State militants buried alive an undefined number of Yazidi women and children, in an attack that killed 500 people, in what has been described as ongoing genocide in northern Iraq.
- *11 August:* The Arab League accused the Islamic State of committing crimes against humanity. The UK decided not to join the US in airstrikes and instead stepped up its humanitarian aid to the refugees.

- *12 August:* The US announced that it would not extend its airstrikes against the Islamic State to areas outside northern Iraq, emphasizing that the objective of the airstrikes was to protect US diplomats in Erbil. The US and the UK airdropped 60,000 litres of water and 75,000 meals. The Vatican called on religious leaders of all denominations, particularly Muslim, to unite and condemn IS for what it described as "heinous crimes" and the use of religion to justify them.
- *13 August:* Jihadists from the Islamic State (IS) group have taken control of a string of villages in the northern Syrian province of Aleppo, a monitoring group said on Wednesday.The Britain-based Syrian Observatory for Human Rights said the extremist group had managed to seize the six villages north of the city of Aleppo, and not far from the border with Turkey."
- *14 August:* Brochures urging Muslims to leave Britain and join ISIS were handed out to shoppers in Oxford Street in central London. Men were described as standing in front of posters declaring "the dawn of a new era has begun" and handing out pro-ISIS brochures. "The khilafah (Caliphate) has been established", one leaflet read, in reference to territories gained in Iraq and Syria after ISIS waged its lightning offensive in recent weeks. Another leaflet said: "We have been living in a constant state of ignorance, our lands separated, resources stolen, ummah disunited, honour humiliated and the laws of shirk established over us."
- 15 August: The United Nations Security Council issued a resolution which "deplores and condemns in the strongest terms the terrorist acts of ISIL (Islamic State) and its violent extremist ideology, and its continued gross, systematic and widespread abuses of human rights and violations of international humanitarian law."
- 16 August: The Islamic State massacred 80 Yazidis. The EU agreed to supply Kurdish forces with arms, and US military forces continued to attack Islamic State fighters in the area around Iraq's crucial Mosul Dam.

- 17 August: The Syrian Observatory for Human Rights reported that the Islamic State had killed 700 members of the Syrian al-Sheitaat tribe, mostly civilians, after two weeks of clashes over the control of two oilfields in the region. Peshmerga troops, aided by the US air campaign, began an offensive to take back the strategic Mosul Dam from the Islamic State, amid fears that the destruction of the dam might unleash a 65-foot wave of water that could engulf the northern city of Mosul, and even flood Baghdad.
- 18 August: Pope Francis, leader of the world's 1.2 billion Roman Catholics, said that the international community would be justified in stopping Islamist militants in Iraq. He also said that it should not be up to a single nation to decide how to intervene in the conflict.
- 19 August: According to the Syrian Observatory for Human Rights, the Islamic State now has an army of more than 50,000 fighters in Syria. American journalistJames Foley was beheaded by the Islamic State on video tape.
- 20 August: US President Obama denounced the "brutal murder of Jim Foley by the terrorist group ISIL."
- 21 August: The US military admitted that a covert rescue attempt involving dozens of US Special Operations forces had been made to rescue James Foley and other Americans held captive in Syria by Islamic State militants. The air and ground assault, involving the first known US military ground action inside Syria, had the authorization of President Barack Obama. The ensuing gunfight resulted in one US soldier being injured. The rescue was unsuccessful, as Foley and the other captives were not in the location targeted. This was the first known engagement by US ground forces with suspected Islamic State militants. The US Defense Secretary warned that the Islamic State were tremendously well-funded, adding, "They have no standard of decency, of responsible human behavior" and that they were an imminent threat to the US.
- 22 August: The US is considering airstrikes on ISIS in Syria, which would draw US military forces directly into

the Syrian Civil War, as President Obama develops a long-term strategy to defeat the Islamic State.

- 28 August: The Islamic State beheaded a Lebanese Army soldier whom they had kidnapped. The group also beheaded a Kurdish Peshmerga fighter in response to Kurdistan's alliance with the United States, and executed around 250 Syrian soldiers captured after the fall of Tabqa Air Base in Ar-Raqqah province. The soldiers had earlier been marched to their place of execution wearing just their underwear.
- 29 August: UK Prime Minister David Cameron raised its terror level to "severe" and committed to fight radical Islam "at home and abroad".
- 31 August: Iraqi military forces supported by Shia militias and American airstrikes broke the two-month siege of the northern Iraqi town of Amerli by Islamic State militants. German Federal Minister of Defence Ursula von der Leyen announced that Germany will send enough weapons to arm 4,000 Peshmerga fighters in northern Iraq fighting Islamic State insurgents. The delivery to be scheduled in stages will include 16,000 assault rifles, 40 machine guns, 240 rocket-propelled grenades, 500 MILAN anti-tank missiles with 30 launchers and 10,000 hand grenades, with a total value of around 70 million euros. In order to assess the needs of the Peshmerga and prevent an accumulation of excess of arms, the Bundeswehr seconded six liaison officers to Erbil, who will report to Berlin.
- 1 September: The German government's Cabinet decision to arm the Kurdish Peshmerga militia was ratified in the Bundestag by a "vast majority" of votes, after an emotional debate.

2013 events:

- Starting in April 2013, the group made rapid military gains in controlling large parts of Northern Syria, where the Syrian Observatory for Human Rights described them as "the strongest group".

- *11 May:* Two car bombs exploded in the town of Reyhanlý in Hatay Province, Turkey. At least 51 people were killed and 140 injured in the attack. The attack was the deadliest single act of terrorism ever to take place on Turkish soil. Along with the Syrian intelligence service, ISIS was suspected of carrying out the bombing attack.
- By 12 May, nine Turkish citizens, who were alleged to have links with Syria's intelligence service, had been detained. On 21 May 2013, the Turkish authorities charged the prime suspect, according to the state-run Anatolia news agency. Four other suspects were also charged and 12 people had been charged in total. All suspects were Turkish nationals whom Ankara believed were backed by the Syrian government.
- In July, Free Syrian Army battalion chief Kamal Hamami—better known by his nom de guerre Abu Bassir Al-Jeblawi—was killed by the group's Coastal region emir after his convoy was stopped at an ISIS checkpoint in Latakia's rural northern highlands. Al-Jeblawi was traveling to visit the Al-Izz Bin Abdulsalam Brigade operating in the region when ISIS members refused his passage, resulting in an exchange of fire in which Al-Jeblawi received a fatal gunshot wound.
- Also in July, ISIS organised a mass break-out of its members being held in Iraq's Abu Ghraib prison. British newspaper *The Guardian* reported that over 500 prisoners escaped, including senior commanders of the group. ISIS issued an online statement claiming responsibility for the prison break, describing the operation as involving 12 car bombs, numerous suicide bombers and mortar and rocket fire. It was described as the culmination of a one-year campaign called "destroying the walls", which was launched on 21 July 2012 by ISIS leader Abu Bakr al-Baghdadi; the aim was to replenish the group's ranks with comrades released from the prison.
- In early August, ISIS led the final assault in the Siege of Menagh Air Base.

- In September, members of the group kidnapped and killed the Ahrar ash-Sham commander Abu Obeida Al-Binnishi, after he had intervened to protect members of a Malaysian Islamic charity; ISIS had mistaken their Malaysian flag for that of the United States.
- Also in September, ISIS overran the Syrian town of Azaz, taking it from an FSA-affiliated rebel brigade. ISIS members had attempted to kidnap a German doctor working in Azaz. In November 2013, *Today's Zaman*, an English-language newspaper in Turkey, reported that Turkish authorities were on high alert, with the authorities saying that they had detailed information on ISIS's plans to carry out suicide bombings in major cities in Turkey, using seven explosive-laden cars being constructed in Ar-Raqqah.
- From 30 September, several Turkish media web sites reported that ISIS had accepted responsibility for the attack and had threatened further attacks on Turkey.
- In November, the Syrian Observatory for Human Rights stated: "ISIS is the strongest group in Northern Syria—100 per cent—and anyone who tells you anything else is lying."
- In December, there were reports of fighting between ISIS and another Islamic rebel group, Ahrar ash-Sham, in the town of Maskana, Aleppo in Syria.

2009–12 events:

- In the 25 October 2009 Baghdad bombings 155 people were killed and at least 721 were injured, and in the 8 December 2009 Baghdad bombings at least 127 people were killed and 448 were injured. The ISI claimed responsibility for both attacks.
- The ISI claimed responsibility for the 25 January 2010 Baghdad bombings that killed 41 people, and the 4 April 2010 Baghdad bombings that killed 42 people and injured 224. On 17 June 2010, the group claimed responsibility for an attack on the Central Bank of Iraq that killed 18 people and wounded 55. On 19 August 2010, in a statement posted on a web site often used by Islamist radicals, the ISI claimed responsibility for the 17 August 2010 Baghdad bombings.

It also claimed responsibility for the bombings in October 2010.

- According to the SITE Institute, the ISI claimed responsibility for the 2010 Baghdad church attack that took place during a Sunday Mass on 31 October 2010.
- *8 February 2011:* According to the SITE Institute, a statement of support for Egyptian protesters—which appears to have been the first reaction of any group affiliated with al-Qaeda to the protests in Egypt during the 2011 Arab Spring Movement—was issued by the Islamic State of Iraq on jihadist forums. The message addressed to the protesters was that the "market of jihad" had opened in Egypt, that "the doors of martyrdom had opened", and that every able-bodied man must participate. It urged Egyptians to ignore the "ignorant deceiving ways" of secularism, democracy and "rotten pagan nationalism". "Your jihad", it went on, is in support of Islam and the weak and oppressed in Egypt, for "your people" in Gaza and Iraq, and "for every Muslim" who has been "touched by the oppression of the tyrant of Egypt and his masters in Washington and Tel Aviv".
- In a four-month process ending in October 2011, the Syrian government reportedly released imprisoned Islamic radicals and provided them with arms "in order to make itself the least bad choice for the international community."
- *23 July 2012:* About 32 attacks occurred across Iraq, killing 116 people and wounding 299. The ISI claimed responsibility for the attacks, which took the form of bombings and shootings.

2007 events:

- Between late 2006 and May 2007, the ISI brought the Dora neighbourhood of southern Baghdad under its control. Numerous Christian families left, unwilling to pay the jizya tax. US efforts to drive out the ISI presence stalled in late June 2007, despite streets being walled off and the use of biometric identification technology. By November 2007, the ISI had been removed from Dora, and Assyrian churches could be re-opened. In 2007 alone the ISI killed around 2,000 civilians, making that year the most violent in its campaign against the civilian population of Iraq.

- *9 March:* The Interior Ministry of Iraq said that Abu Omar al-Baghdadi had been captured in Baghdad, but it was later said that the person in question was not al-Baghdadi.
- *19 April:* The organization announced that it had set up a provisional government termed "the first Islamic administration" of post-invasion Iraq. The "emirate" was stated to be headed by Abu Omar al-Baghdadi and his "cabinet" of ten "ministers".

The names listed above are all considered to be noms de guerre:

- *3 May:* Iraqi sources claimed that Abu Omar al-Baghdadi had been killed a short time earlier. According to the *The Long War Journal*, no evidence was provided to support this and US sources remained skeptical. The Islamic State of Iraq released a statement later that day which denied his death.
- *12 May:* In what was apparently the same incident, it was announced that "Minister of Public Relations" Abu Bakr al-Jabouri had been killed on 12 May 2007 near Taji. The exact circumstances of the incident remain unknown. The initial version of the events at Taji, as given by the Iraqi Interior Ministry, was that there had been a shoot-out between rival Sunni militias. Coalition and Iraqi government operations were apparently being conducted in the same area at about the same time and later sources implied that they were directly involved, with al-Jabouri being killed while resisting arrest.
- *12 May:* The ISI issued a press release claiming responsibility for an ambush at Al Taqa, Babil on 12 May 2007, in which one Iraqi soldier and four US 10th Mountain Division soldiers were killed. Three soldiers of the US unit were captured and one was found dead in the Euphrates 11 days later. After a 4,000-man hunt by the US and allied forces ended without success, the ISI released a video in which it was claimed that the other two soldiers had been

executed and buried, but no direct proof was given. Their bodies were found a year later.

- *18 June:* The US launched Operation Arrowhead Ripper, as "a large-scale effort to eliminate Al-Qaeda in Iraq terrorists operating in Baquba and its surrounding areas".
- *25 June:* The suicide bombing of a meeting of Al Anbar tribal leaders and officials at Mansour Hotel, Baghdad killed 13 people, including six Sunni sheikhs and other prominent figures. This was proclaimed by the ISI to have been in retaliation for the rape of a Sunni woman by Iraqi police. Security at the hotel, which is 100 meters outside the Green Zone, was provided by a British contractor which had apparently hired guerrilla fighters to provide physical security. There were allegations that an Egyptian Islamist group may have been responsible for the bombing, but this has never been proven.
- In July, Abu Omar al-Baghdadi released an audio tape in which he issued an ultimatum to Iran. He said: "We are giving the Persians, and especially the rulers of Iran, a two-month period to end all kinds of support for the Iraqi Shia government and to stop direct and indirect intervention... otherwise a severe war is waiting for you." He also warned Arab states against doing business with Iran. Iran supports the Iraqi government which many see as anti-Sunni.
- Resistance to coalition operations in Baqubah turned out to be less than anticipated. In early July, US Army sources suggested that any ISI leadership in the area had largely relocated elsewhere in early June 2007, before the start of Operation Arrowhead Ripper.

2003–06 events:

- The group was founded in 2003 as a reaction to the American-led invasion and occupation of Iraq. Its first leader was the Jordanian militant Abu Musab al-Zarqawi, who declared allegiance to Osama bin Laden's al-Qaeda network on 17 October 2004. Foreign fighters from outside Iraq were thought to play a key role in its network. The group became a primary target of the Iraqi government and its foreign supporters, and attacks between these groups resulted in more than 1,000 deaths every year between 2004 and 2010.

- The Islamic State of Iraq made clear its belief that targeting civilians was an acceptable strategy and it has been responsible for thousands of civilian deaths since 2004. In September 2005, al-Zarqawi declared war on Shia Muslims and the group used bombings—especially suicide bombings in public places—massacres and executions to carry out terrorist attacks on Shia-dominated and mixed sectarian neighbourhoods. Suicide attacks by the ISI also killed hundreds of Sunni civilians, which engendered widespread anger among Sunnis.

ISLAMIC STATE OF IRAQ AND ASH SHAM / ISLAMIC STATE (ISLAMIC STATE OF IRAQ, ISIS OR ISIL, IS)

The ISIS was preceded by the Islamic State of Iraq (ISI), that was established during October 2006, and comprised of various insurgent groups, most significantly the original Al Qaeda Organization in the Land of the Two Rivers (AQI) organization, al-Qaeda in Mesopotami - led by Abu Musab al-Zarqawi, the Mujahedeen Shura Council in Iraq, and Jund al-Sahhaba (Soldiers of the Prophet's Companions), which was integrated into the ISI. ISIS members' allegiance was given to the ISI commander and not al-Qaeda central command. The organisation known as the ISIS was formed during April 2013 and has evolved in one of the main jihadist groups fighting government forces in Syria and Iraq. ISIS regards Baquba, Iraq, as its headquarters with its allegiance to Abu Omar al-Baghdadi as the group's emir. Baghdadi's real name is Hamed Dawood Mohammed Khalil al-Zawi.

Rifts Between ISIS and Other Terror and Rebel Groups

The ISIS has extensive financial resources (mostly derived from alleged organised crime activities in areas of control as well as diaspora funds and unidentified financial sponsors from within Gulf states) as well as human capital that enable operations in various locations. This is seen in attacks executed in areas regarded as primarily Shi'a areas in Iraq, such as Najaf, Karbala, Kut and

Wasit as well as bombings in Baghdad (Iraq). These attacks also reflected sophistication both in terms of execution and diverse tactics. More recent skirmishes with Iraqi government forces are evidence of an extensive ISIS capacity.

Objective/Goal

The ISIS's objective is the establishment of a world wide Caliphate, reflected in frequent media reports by means of images of the world united under a ISIS banner. Although it has perpetrated many terrorist acts since its formation in 2006, especially against Shia and Christian civilians, ISI/ISIS/ISIL has been especially active in late 2102 and 2013, claiming responsibility for killing and wounding hundreds of people through suicide bombings. It's principal targets are U.S. military and Shia and Christian civilians.

ISIS LEADERSHIP STRUCTURE (2014)

ISIS Organisational Structure in Iraq and Syria

The ISIS is composed of 16 wilayats (read provinces/ administrative districts), in both Iraq and Syria and is reflected in the following map:

LIST OF AREAS THE ISLAMIC STATE CLAIMS IT CONTROLS AFTER THIS WEEK'S OFFENSIVE IN NINEWA, FROM AUG. 7, 2014 STATEMENT ON TWITTER:

1. All of Sinjar municipality and the areas belonging to it.
2. All of Talkif municipality and the areas belonging to it.
3. All of al-Hamdaniya municipality and the areas belonging to it.
4. All of Makhmour municipality and the areas belonging to it.
5. Zammar township and all the villages belonging to it.
6. Rabee'ah township and all the villages belonging to it.
7. Bartala township and all the villages belonging to it.
8. Karam Lays township and all the villages belonging to it.
9. Al-Kweir township and all the villages belonging to it.
10. Wana township and all the villages belonging to it.

11. Large areas in Filfeel township.
12. Large areas of Ba'ashiqa township.
13. Some of the al-Shalalat areas in Mosul.
14. The Sada and Ba'wiza area of Mosul.
15. The oil-rich 'Ayn Zalah area.
16. The strategic Mosul dam
17. The large Tumarat base.

THE ISLAMIC STATE OF IRAQ AND THE SHAM'S 16 WILAYATS ARE:

IN IRAQ:

- Southern Division (based in Babil province, south of Baghdad)
- Diyala Division
- Baghdad Division
- Kirkuk Division
- Salahuddin Division
- Anbar Division (is the largest and most active wilayat in Iraq)
- Ninewa Division

IN SYRIA:

- Al Barakah Division (Hasaka)
- Al Kheir Division (Deir al Zour)
- Al Raqqah Division
- Al Badiya Division
- Halab [Aleppo] Division
- Idlib Division
- Hama Division
- Damascus Division
- Coast [Al Sahel] Division

Areas of Operation in Iraq

Anbar Province

The ISIS stronghold is in the Anbar province, as seen in the operation of training camps coupled with attacks on Government security personnel, a case in point being various suicide bomb attacks in a single day targeting local police in Rawa. In addition, the ISIS gained control in areas of Ramadi and Fallujah, following the withdrawal of the Iraqi army due to widespread Sunni rejection of attempts to dismantle the Ramadi camp protest site. Their presence in these areas were also seen in Anbar with mortar attacks at the Sahwa leader Abu Risha's estate and fighting with security forces in various Anbar urban locations, such as the al-Mal'ab quarter in Ramadi and the al-Khaldiya area near Fallujah.

Mosul, Baiji, Babil, and Baghdad

Beyond Anbar, the group has enacted frequent attacks on the Iraqi army in various districts of Mosul as well as target specific bomb attacks in the Baiji area of Salah ad-Din province, Jurf al-Sakhr in northern Babil province (just south of Baghdad), and the Tarmiya area of northern Baghdad province, where assaults have been launched on "Sahwa" forces, resulting in incidents such as the execution of 18 Sunnis suspected of being "Sahwa militia" during November 2013.

Kurdistan

During 2013, ISIS operations expanded to Iraqi Kurdistan, as seen in the Arbil bombings in September 2013, that the ISIS referred to as retaliation due to the Kurdistan Regional Government's alleged support for the "PKK" in Syria.

ISIS in Syria

In April 2013, ISIS attempted to morph into the creation of the Islamic State of Iraq and the Levant (ISIS/ISIL) but the formation of a new group was rejected by the al-Nusra Front. ISIS's leader, Abu Bakr al-Baghdadi, known as Abu Dua, nevertheless pressed ahead with expanding its operations into Syria. In August 2013, US intelligence assessed that he was based in Syria and commanded as many 5,000 fighters, many of them foreign jihadists. The group is active mostly in northern and eastern provinces of Syria. It has assumed joint control of municipalities in Aleppo, Idlib and Raqqa provinces. In November 2013 Al-Qaeda chief Ayman al-Zawahiri ordered the disbanding of the main jihadist faction in Syria, the

ISIL, in an audio message aired on Al-Jazeera. The tape appeared to confirm a letter posted by Al-Jazeera in June 2013, claimed to have been written by Zawahiri and addressed to the leaders of Al-Qaeda factions in both countries. The head of Al-Qaeda also stressed that the Al-Nusra Front was the branch of the global jihadist group in Syria.ISIL's extremism has resulted in the deaths of more than 1,000 rebels in the last 3-4 weeks alone.

ISIS in Lebanon

The ISIS reach into Lebanon is seen in the following most recent developments:

On 3 January 2014, a leader in the Jordanian Salafi movement said the ISIS has decided officially to infiltrate Lebanon militarily, by stating that "the leader of al-Nusra Front Abu Muhammad al-Goulani and the prince of "ISIL" Abu Baker al-Baghdadi have decided to enter Lebanon militarily".

The ISIS claimed credit for the suicide bombing Haret Hreik in the southern suburb of Beirut on 22 January 2014, which killed 5 people. In the statement released via Twitter, the ISIS stated that the group has the capacity to violate Hezbollah security measures and that the suicide bombing is "a first small payment from the heavy account that is awaiting those criminals."

The above announcement was followed by the Lebanon-focused A'isha Media Center announcement of an online campaign to support the ISIS in the conflict with Syrian militant factions.

On 25 January 2013 a video recording declared the creation of a Lebanese division for the ISIS. In the recording, Abu Sayyaf al-Ansari (further details unknown) swears allegiance to Abu Bakr al-Baghdadi, the Iraqi leader of ISIS. He also called on Sunnis to abandon the Lebanese crusader" army, supportive of continued allegations by Sunni Islamists that the armed forces are "backed by Hezbollah." The recording surfaced amid escalating tensions in Lebanon linked to the war in neighbouring Syria. While the Lebanon's Shiite Hezbollah has deployed troops to Syria to back President Bashar al-Assad, many Sunnis are opposed to Assad and any support to his government. In the five-minute recording, al-Ansari indicated that "a spokesman for ISIS in Lebanon" identified as Abu Omar al-Muhajir would soon make a statement of his own.

ISIS in Gaza Strip/West Bank

During February 2014, the ISIS released a video that showed ISIS fighters announcing plans to wage a jihad in Gaza. A spokesperson in the video announced that DAESH (ISIS) now has "lions and armies in the environs of Jerusalem" and called on Muslims to support the group in their jihad against the enemies of Islam and "Arab tyrants." The ISIS regards Hamas as to moderate and not committed in the fight against Israel. The ISIS announcement is the first indication of presence within Gaza Strip/ West Bank as well as a direct challenge to the Palestinian Islamist movement Hamas. The extent of support for the ISIS from Gaza culminated in the formation of an ISIS Syrian brigade comprised and dedicated to fighters from Gaza, referred to as the "Sheikh Abu al-Nur al-Maqdisi Brigade," named after the founder of the Jund Ansar Allah group in Gaza- Abdel Latif Moussa, who was killed in clashes with Hamas in 2009.

2

Historical Background of Islamic State in Iraq and Syria

INTRODUCTION

Islamic State in Iraq and Syria (ISIS), a predominantly Sunni jihadist group, seeks to sow civil unrest in Iraq and the Levant with the aim of establishing a caliphate—a single, transnational Islamic state based on sharia. The group emerged in the ashes of the U.S.-led invasion to oust Saddam Hussein as al-Qaeda in Iraq (AQI), and the insurgency that followed provided it with fertile ground to wage a guerrilla war against coalition forces and their domestic allies.

After a U.S. counterterrorism campaign and Sunni efforts to maintain local security in what was known as the Tribal Awakening, AQI violence diminished from its peak in 2006–2007. But since the withdrawal of U.S. forces in late 2011, the group has increased attacks on mainly Shiite targets in what is seen as an attempt to reignite conflict between Iraq's Sunni minority and the Shiite-dominated government of Prime Minister Nouri al-Maliki.

Burgeoning violence in 2013 left nearly eight thousand civilians dead, making it Iraq's bloodiest year since 2008, according to the United Nations. Meanwhile, in 2012 the group adopted its new moniker, ISIS (sometimes translated as Islamic State of Iraq and the Levant, or ISIL) as an expression of its broadened ambitions as its fighters have crossed into neighboring Syria to challenge both the Assad regime and secular and Islamist opposition groups there. By June 2014, the group's fighters had routed the Iraqi military in the major cities of Fallujah and Mosul and established territorial control and administrative structures on both sides of the Iraqi-Syrian border.

Origins

The insurgent group was launched by Abu Musab al-Zarqawi, an Arab of Jordanian descent, and flourished in the sectarian tensions that followed the U.S.-led invasion of Iraq in 2003. Zarqawi had commanded volunteers in Herat, Afghanistan, before fleeing to northern Iraq in 2001. There he joined with Ansar al-Islam (Partisans of Islam), a militant Kurdish separatist movement, for whom he led the group's Arab contingent. Analysts say this group, not al-Qaeda, was the precursor to AQI.

Ahead of the 2003 invasion, U.S. officials made a case before the UN Security Council linking Zarqawi's group with Osama bin Laden, though some experts say it wasn't until October 2004 that Zarqawi vowed obedience to the al-Qaeda leader. The U.S. State Department designated AQI a foreign terrorist organization that same month. "For al-Qaeda, attaching its name to Zarqawi's activities enabled it to maintain relevance even as its core forces were destroyed [in Afghanistan] or on the run," wrote Brian Fishman, a counterterrorism fellow at the New America Foundation.

According to a 2011 report by the Center for Strategic and International Studies, Zarqawi developed a four-pronged strategy[PDF] to defeat the coalition: isolate U.S. forces by targeting its allies; discourage Iraqi collaboration by targeting government infrastructure and personnel; target reconstruction efforts through high-profile attacks on civilian contractors and aid workers; and draw the U.S. military into a Sunni-Shiite civil war by targeting Shiites.

The Coalition Provisional Authority (CPA), the transitional government established by the United States and its coalition partners, made two decisions early in the U.S.-led occupation that are often cited as having fed the insurgency. The CPA's first order banned members of Saddam Hussein's Ba'ath party from government positions (so-called "de-Baathification"); its second order disbanded the Iraqi army and security services, creating hundreds of thousands of new coalition enemies, many of them armed Sunnis.

"For al-Qaeda, attaching its name to Zarqawi's activities enabled it to maintain relevance even as its core forces were destroyed [in Afghanistan] or on the run." —Brian Fishman, New America Foundation

AQI's fighters were drawn initially from Zarqawi's networks [PDF] in Pakistan and Afghanistan, and later merged with recruits from Syria, Iraq, and its neighbors. The group's makeup became predominantly Iraqi by 2006, the *Washington Post* reported. But while the group peaked in 2006 and 2007 at the height of Iraq's sectarian civil war—which AQI helped foment—its ranks were diminished by a counterterrorism campaign by U.S. Special Operations Forces and the U.S.-backed Sahwa, or Sunni Awakening movement.

Leadership

Osama bin Laden and Zawahiri believed AQI's indiscriminate attacks on fellow Muslims would erode public support for al-Qaeda in the region, and in July 2005 they questioned Zarqawi's strategy in written correspondence. Fishman said the relationship collapsed when Zarqawi ignored al-Qaeda instructions to stop attacking Shiite cultural sites.

A U.S. air strike that killed Zarqawi in June 2006 marked a victory for U.S. and Iraqi intelligence and a turning point for AQI. In its aftermath, Abu Ayyub al-Masri, an Egyptian-born explosives expert and former Zawahiri confidant, emerged as AQI's new leader. In October 2006, Masri adopted the alias Islamic State of Iraq (ISI) to increase the group's local appeal, which suffered just as Zawahiri had feared, and embody its territorial ambitions; it later came to be known as ISIS, reflecting its broadened ambitions as instability in neighboring Syria after the 2011 uprising there created new opportunities to exploit. ISIS is currently led by Abu Bakr al-Baghdadi, also known as Abu Du'a. The U.S. government believes he resides in Syria.

Funding

Supporters in the region, including those based in Jordan, Syria, and Saudi Arabia, are believed to have provided the bulk of past FUNDING. Iran has also financed AQI, crossing sectarian lines, as Tehran saw an opportunity to challenge the U.S. military presence in the region, according to the U.S. Treasury and documents confiscated in 2006 from Iranian Revolutionary Guards operatives in northern Iraq. In early 2014, Iran OFFERED to join the United States in offering aid to the Iraqi government to counter al-Qaeda gains in Anbar province.

The bulk of ISIS's financing, experts say, comes from sources such as smuggling, extortion, and other crime. ISIS has relied in recent years on funding and manpower from internal recruits [PDF]. Even prior to ISIS's takeover of Mosul, Iraq's second-largest city, in June 2014, the group extorted taxes from businesses small and large, netting upwards of $8 million a month, according to some estimates.

Staying Power

Heavy-handed actions taken by Maliki to consolidate power in the wake of the U.S. withdrawal have alienated much of the Sunni minority, and ISIS has since exploited the "failed social contract," said former CFR press fellow Ned Parker. Maliki's Shiite-dominated government was reluctant to integrate Awakening militias into the national security forces, and critics say he has persecuted Sunni political rivals and stoked sectarian polarization for political gain.

Sunnis who felt marginalized by the Maliki government began protesting for reforms in Anbar province in December 2012, andprominent Shiite clerics such as the Grand Ayatollah Ali Sistani and Moqtada al-Sadr acknowledged the legitimacy of their grievances, Parker wrote. According to a report by the nonpartisan Congressional Research Service [PDF], there were roughly a dozen days in 2012 on which ISIS executed multi-city attacks that killed at least twenty-five Iraqis. On at least four of those days, coordinated attacks left more than a hundred Iraqis dead.

In April 2013, Iraqi security forces raided a protest camp at al-Hawijah, provoking an escalation in Sunni militancy. Car bombings and suicide attacks intensified, with coordinated attacks regularly targeting Shiite MARKETS, cafes, and mosques.

In 2013, 7,818 civilians (including police) were killed in acts of terrorism and violence, more than double the 2012 death toll, according to United Nations figures. An additional 17,891 were injured, making 2013 Iraq's bloodiest year since 2008. At the end of 2013, security forces sought to clear a protest camp in Ramadi. The move provoked an uprising in which security forces pulled out of the city as well as nearby Fallujah, and ISIS moved to fill the void.

Meanwhile, the civil war in neighboring Syria has drawn Sunni jihadists into the rebellion against the regime of Bashar al-Assad, which is dominated by the Alawite sect, an offshoot of Shiite Islam.

While al-Qaeda-linked groups in Syria have fought among themselves and with the secular opposition, the Free Syrian Armysigned a truce with ISIS in late September, an acknowledgment of their efficacy on the battlefield. But divisions within the Islamist opposition camp remain stark.

ISIS declared a merger with Jabhat al-Nusra, an al-Qaeda affiliate that has greater indigenous legitimacy in Syria, in April 2013. But Zawahiri, who succeeded bin Laden as head of so-called "core al-Qaeda," annulled the merger, ruling that Baghdadi's group's operations be limited to Iraq. Baghdadi rejected Zawahiri's ruling and questioned his authority, his group's pledge of fealty to al-Qaeda notwithstanding. Various rival Islamist militant groups coalesced in late 2013 as the Mujahedeen Army with the common goal of forcing ISIS to cede territory and leave Syria.

At odds with al-Qaeda's aims, ISIS has since expanded its territorial control, establishing a "de facto state in the borderlands of Syria and Iraq" that exhibits some of the traditional markers of sovereignty, note Douglas A. Ollivant and Fishman. Beyond fielding a militia, it provides limited services and administers its ultraconservative brand of justice. Much of Anbar province has remained outside the central government's authority since January

2014, and in mid-2014, a Sunni insurgency wrested control of Mosul and its environs after the predominantly Shiite army, hobbled by desertions and cronyism, retreated overnight. ISIS is at the vanguard of the insurgency, but the tactical alliances it has formed with non-jihadi Sunnis, including former members of the Ba'athist regime, have led analysts and policymakers to question how long it can rule over a population concerned by ISIS's extremism.

The takeovers highlighted Baghdad's weakness: In Fallujah, Maliki called on Sunni tribesmen to resist ISIS, and in Mosul, which had been considered a model for the surge and Awakening, he called on the Kurdish security forces, the peshmerga, to do the same. Maliki has also mobilized Shiite militias implicated in sectarian killings, and Iraqi forces are accused of indiscriminate airstrikes. Meanwhile, ISIS gains in the country's north set back the peshmerga and have created a humanitarian crisis for thousands of Iraqi Christians and Yezidis, who are among religious and ethnic minorities targeted by ISIS.

Insurgents' consolidation of territorial control is a concern for the United States, which believes such areas outside of state authority may become safe havens for those jihadis with ambitions oriented toward the "far enemy"—the West. The Obama administration has responded to the regional resurgence by increasing the CIA's support for the Maliki government, including assistance to elite counterterrorism units that report directly to the prime minister, and providing Hellfire missiles and surveillance drones. After Iraqi forces retreated from Mosul, the insurgents who routed them released more than one thousandprisoners and picked up troves of U.S.-supplied matériel.

ISLAMIC STATE.

An Islamic state is a type of government, in which the primary basis for government is Islamic religious law (*sharia*). From the early years of Islam, numerous governments have been founded as "Islamic", beginning most notably with thecaliphate established by Muhammad himself and including subsequent governments ruled under the direction of a caliph (meaning "successor" to the Islamic prophet Muhammad).

However, the term "Islamic state" has taken on a more specific modern connotation since the 18th century. The concept of the modern Islamic state has been articulated and promoted by ideologues such as Abul A'la Maududi, Ayatollah Ruhollah Khomeini, Israr Ahmed, and Sayyid Qutb. Like the earlier notion of the caliphate, the modern Islamic state is rooted in Islamic law. It is modeled after the rule of Muhammad. However, unlike caliph-led governments which were imperial despotisms or monarchies (Arabic: *malik*), a modern Islamic state can incorporate modern political institutions such as elections, parliamentary rule, judicial review, and popular sovereignty.

Today, many Muslim countries have incorporated Islamic law, wholly or in part, into their legal systems. Certain Muslim states have declared Islam to be their state religion in theirconstitutions, but do not apply Islamic law in their courts. Islamic states which are not Islamic monarchies are usually referred to as Islamic republics.

THE HISTORICAL ISLAMIC STATE

Early Islamic Governments

The term caliphate refers to the first system of government established by Muhammad in 622 CE, under the Constitution of Medina. It represented the political unity of the Muslim *Ummah*(nation), although it did not always incorporate the full religious community of Muslims (for example, Khawarijites and Shia). It was subsequently led by Muhammad's disciples who were known as the Rightly Guided (*Rashidun*) Caliphs (632-661 CE). The Arabian Empire significantly expanded under the Umayyad Caliphate (622-750) and the Abbasid Caliphate (750-1258).

The Essence of Islamic Governments

The essence or guiding principles of an Islamic government or Islamic state, is the concept of*Al-Shura*. Different scholars have different understandings or thoughts, with regard to the concept al-Shura, However, most Muslim scholars are of the opinion that Islamic al-Shura should consist of:

- Meeting or consultation, that follows the teachings of Islam.
- Consultation following the guidelines of the *Quran* and *Sunnah*.
- There is a leader elected among them to head the meeting.
- The discussion should be based on *mushawarah* and *mudhakarah*.
- All the members are given fair opportunity to voice out their opinions.
- The issue should be of *maslahah ammah* or public interest.
- The voices of the majority are accepted, provided that it does not violate with the teachings of the Quran or Sunnah.

Muhammad himself respected the decision of the shura members. He is the champion of the notion of al-shura, and this was illustrated in one of the many historical events, such as, in the Battle of Khandaq (Battle of the Trench), where Muhammad was faced with two decisions, i.e. to fight the invading pagan Arabs outside of Medina or wait till they enter the city. After consultation with the *sahabah*(companions), it was suggested by Salman al-Farsi that it would be better if the Muslims fought the unbelievers within Medina by building a big ditch on the northern periphery of Medina to prevent the enemies from entering Medina. This idea was later supported by the majority of the sahabah, and thereafter Muhammad also approved it.

The reason why Muhammad placed great emphasis on the agreement of the decision of the shura, was because the majority of opinion (by the sahabah) is better than the decision made by one individual.

Revival and Abolition of the Ottoman Caliphate

The Ottoman Sultan, Selim I (1512–1520) reclaimed the title of caliph, which had been in dispute and asserted by a diversity of rulers and "shadow caliphs" in the centuries of the Abbasid-Mamluk Caliphate since the Mongols' sacking of Baghdad and the killing of the last Abbasid Caliph in Baghdad, Iraq 1258.

The Ottoman Caliphate as an office of the Ottoman Empire was abolished under Mustafa Kemal Atatürk in 1924 as part of

Atatürk's Reforms. This move was most vigorously protested in India, as Gandhi and Indian Muslims united behind the *symbolism* of the Ottoman Caliph in the Khilafat (or "Caliphate") Movement, which sought to reinstate the Caliph deposed by Atatürk. The Khilafat Movement leveraged the Ottoman political resistance to the British Empire, and this international anti-imperial connection proved to be a galvanizing force duringIndia's nascent nationalism movement of the early 1900s, for Hindus and Muslims alike, even though India was far from the seat of the Ottoman Caliphate in Istanbul.

THE MODERN ISLAMIC STATE

Origins in 20th-century Nationalist and Anti-imperialist Movements

"The very term, 'Islamic State', was never used in the theory or practice of Muslim political science, before the twentieth century," a Pakistani scholar wrote, and western scholars of Islam agree. The modern conceptualization of the "Islamic state" is attributed to Abul A'la Maududi (1903–1979), a Pakistani Muslim theologian who founded the political party Jamaat-e-Islami and inspired other Islamic revolutionaries such as Ayatollah Ruhollah Khomeini. Abul A'la Maududi's early political career was influenced greatly by anti-colonial agitation in India, especially after the tumultuous abolition of the Ottoman Caliphate in 1924 stoked anti-British sentiment.

The Islamic state was perceived as a "third way" between the rival political systems of democracy and socialism. Maududi's seminal writings on Islamic economics argued as early as 1941 against free-market capitalism and socialist state intervention in the economy, similar to Mohammad Baqir al-Sadr's later *Our Economics* written in 1961. Maududi envisioned the ideal Islamic state as combining the democratic principles of electoral politics with the socialist principles of concern for the poor.

Islamic States Today

Today, many Muslim countries have incorporated Islamic law, wholly or in part, into their legal systems. Certain Muslim states have declared Islam to be their state religion in their constitutions, but do not apply Islamic law in their courts. Islamic states which are not Islamic monarchies are usually referred to as Islamic republics, including the Islamic Republics of Pakistan, Iran and Afghanistan. Pakistan adopted the title under the constitution of 1956. Mauritania adopted it on 28 November 1958. Iran adopted it after the 1979 Revolution that overthrew the Pahlavi dynasty. In Iran, the form of government is known as "Guardianship of the Islamic Jurists". Afghanistan was run as an Islamic state ("Islamic State of Afghanistan") in the post-communist era since 1992 but then de facto by the Taliban ("Islamic Emirate of Afghanistan") in areas controlled by them since 1996, and after the 2001 overthrow of the Taliban the country is still known as the "Islamic Republic of Afghanistan". Despite the similar name, the countries differ greatly in their governments and laws.

Pan-Islamism is a form of religious nationalism within political Islam which advocates the unification of the Muslim world under a single Islamic state, often described as a caliphate.

The Libyan interim Constitutional Declaration of 3 August 2011 declared Islam to be the official religion of Libya.

MODERN WORLD ISLAMIC STATES

Iran

Leading up to the Iranian Revolution of 1979, many of the highest-ranking clergy in Shia Islam held to the standard doctrine of the Imamate, which allows political rule only by Muhammad or one of his true successors. They were opposed to creating an Islamic state. Contemporary theologians who were once part of the Iranian Revolution also became disenchanted and critical of the unity of religion and state in the Islamic Republic of Iran, are advocating secularization of the state to preserve the purity of the Islamic faith.

Pakistan

Pakistan was created as a separate state for Indian Muslims in British India in 1947, and followed the parliamentary form of democracy. In 1949, the first Constituent Assembly of Pakistan passed the Objectives Resolution which envisaged an official role for Islam as the state religion to make sure any future law should not violate its basic teachings. On the whole, the state retained most of the laws that were inherited from the secular British legal code that had been enforced by the British Raj since the 19th century. In 1956, the elected parliament formally adopted the name "Islamic Republic of Pakistan", declaring Islam as the official religion.

Islamic State comprising Parts of Iraq and Syria

The Islamic State of Iraq and the Levant (ISIL), alternately translated as the Islamic State of Iraq and Syria (ISIS) or the Islamic State of Iraq and al-Sham, also known by the Arabic acronym *DAISH*, now called simply the Islamic State (IS), is an unrecognized state and active jihadist militant group in Iraq and Syria. This Islamic State of Iraq and the Levant was declared on 29 June 2014

AS JAMA'AT AL-TAWHID WAL-JIHAD (1999–2004)

Origins

Jama'at al-Tawhid wal-Jihad (abrreviated JTJ or shortened to *Tawhid and Jihad, Tawhid wal-Jihad,* sometimes *Tawhid al-Jihad, Al Tawhid* or *Tawhid*) was started in 1999 by Abu Musab al-Zarqawi and a combination of foreigners and local Islamist sympathizers. Al-Zarqawi was a Jordanian Salafi Jihadist who had traveled to Afghanistan to fight in the Soviet-Afghan War, but he arrived after the departure of the Soviet troops and soon returned to his homeland. He eventually returned to Afghanistan, running an Islamic militant training camp near Herat.

Al-Zarqawi started the network with the intention of overthrowing the Kingdom of Jordan, which he considered to be un-Islamic according to the four schools of Sunni Islamic jurisprudence. For this purpose he developed numerous contacts and affiliates in several countries. Although it has not been verified, his network may have been involved in the late 1999 plot to bomb the Millennium celebrations in the United States and Jordan. However, al-Zarqawi's operatives were responsible for the assassination of US diplomat Laurence Foley in Jordan in 2002.

Following the US-led invasion of Afghanistan, al-Zarqawi moved westward into Iraq, where he reportedly received medical treatment in Baghdad for an injured leg. It is believed that he developed extensive ties in Iraq with Ansar al-Islam ("Partisans of Islam"), a Kurdish Islamic militant group based in the extreme northeast of the country. Ansar allegedly had ties to Iraqi Intelligence; Saddam Hussein's motivation would have been to use Ansar as a surrogate force to repress secular Kurds fighting for the independence of Kurdistan. In January 2003, Ansar's founder Mullah Krekar denied any connection with Saddam's government.

The consensus of intelligence officials has since been that there were no links whatsoever between al-Zarqawi and Saddam, and that Saddam viewed Ansar al-Islam "as a threat to the regime" and his intelligence officials were spying on the group. The 2006 Senate Report on Pre-war Intelligence on Iraq concluded: "Postwar information indicates that Saddam Hussein attempted, unsuccessfully, to locate and capture al-Zarqawi and that the regime did not have a relationship with, harbor, or turn a blind eye toward al-Zarqawi." According to Michael Weiss, Ansar entered Iraqi Kurdistan through Iran as part of Iran's covert attempts to destabilize Saddam's government.

Following the 2003 US-led invasion of Iraq, JTJ developed into an expanding militant network for the purpose of resisting the coalition occupation forces and their Iraqi allies. It included some of the remnants of Ansar al-Islam and a growing number of foreign fighters. Many foreign fighters arriving in Iraq were initially not associated with the group, but once they were in the country they became dependent on al-Zarqawi's local contacts.

Goals and Tactics

The stated goals of JTJ were: (i) to force a withdrawal of coalition forces from Iraq; (ii) to topple the Iraqi interim government; (iii) to assassinate collaborators with theoccupation regime; (iv) to remove the Shia population and defeat its militias because of its death-squad activities; and (v) to establish subsequently a pure Islamic state. JTJ differed considerably from the other early Iraqi insurgent groups in its tactics. Rather than using only conventional weapons and guerrilla tactics in ambushes against the US and coalition forces, it relied heavily on suicide bombings, often using car bombs. It targeted a wide variety of groups, especially the Iraqi Security Forces and those facilitating the occupation. Groups of workers who have been targeted by JTJ include Iraqi interim officials, Iraqi Shia and Kurdish political and religious figures, the country's Shia Muslim civilians, foreign civilian contractors, and United Nations and humanitarian workers. Al-Zarqawi's militants are also known to have used a wide variety of other tactics, including targeted kidnappings, the planting of improvised explosive devices, and mortar attacks. Beginning in late June 2004, JTJ implemented urban guerrilla-style attacks using rocket-propelled grenades and small arms. They also gained worldwide notoriety for beheading Iraqi and foreign hostages and distributing video recordings of these acts on the Internet.

Activities

JTJ claimed credit for a number of attacks that targeted Iraqi forces and infrastructure, such as the October 2004 ambush and killing of 49 armed Iraqi National Guardrecruits, and for a series of attacks on humanitarian aid agencies such as the International Red Cross and Red Crescent Movement. It conducted numerous attacks againstUS military personnel throughout 2004, and audacious suicide attacks inside the high-security Green Zone perimeter in Baghdad. Al-Zarqawi's men reputedly succeeded in assassinating several leading Iraqi politicians of the early post-Saddam era, and their bomb attack on the United Nations Mission's headquarters in Iraq led the UN country team to relocate to Jordan and continue their work remotely.

The group took either direct responsibility or the blame for many of the early Iraqi insurgent attacks, including the series of high-profile bombings in August 2003, which killed 17 people at the Jordanian embassy in Baghdad, 23 people, including the chief of the United Nations Mission to Iraq Sérgio Vieira de Mello, at the UN headquarters in Baghdad, and at least 86 people, including Ayatollah Sayed Mohammed Baqir al-Hakim, in the Imam Ali Mosque bombing in Najaf. Included here is the November truck bombing, which killed 27 people, mostly Italian paramilitary policemen, at the Italian base in Nasiriyah. The attacks connected with the group in 2004 include the series of bombings in Baghdad and Karbala which killed 178 people during the holy Day of Ashura in March; the failed plot in April to explode chemical bombs in Amman, Jordan, which was said to have been financed by al-Zarqawi's network; a series of suicide boat bombings of the oil pumping stations in the Persian Gulf in April, for which al-Zarqawi took responsibility in a statement published by the Muntada al-Ansar Islamist website; the May car bombassassination of Iraqi Governing Council president Ezzedine Salim at the entrance to the Green Zone in Baghdad; the June suicide car bombing in Baghdad which killed 35 civilians; and the September car bomb which killed 47 police recruits and civilians on Haifa Street in Baghdad.

Foreign civilian hostages abducted by the group in 2004 included: Americans Nick Berg, Eugene Armstrong and Jack Hensley; Turks Durmus Kumdereli, Aytullah Gezmen and Murat Yuce; South Korean Kim Sun-il; Bulgarians Georgi Lazov and Ivaylo Kepov; and Briton Kenneth Bigley. Most of them were beheaded using knives. Al-Zarqawi personally beheaded Berg and Armstrong, but Yuce was shot dead by al-Masri, and Gezmen was released after "repenting."

AS TANZIM QAIDAT AL-JIHAD FI BILAD AL-RAFIDAYN (2004–2006)

Involvement in Iraqi Insurgency

The group officially pledged allegiance to Osama bin Laden's al-Qaeda network in a letter in October 2004 and changed its official name to *Tanzim Qaidat al-Jihad fi Bilad al-Rafidayn*. That same month, the group, now popularly referred to as Al-Qaeda in Iraq (AQI), kidnapped and killed Japanese citizen Shosei Koda. In November, al-Zarqawi's network was the main target of the US Operation Phantom Fury in Fallujah, but its leadership managed to escape the American siege and subsequent storming of the city. In December, in two of its many sectarian attacks, AQI bombed a Shia funeral procession in Najaf and the main bus station in nearby Karbala, killing at least 60 people in those two holy cities of Shia Islam. The group also reportedly took responsibility for the 30 September 2004 Baghdad bombing which killed 41 people, mostly children.

In 2005, AQI largely focused on executing high-profile and coordinated suicide attacks, claiming responsibility for numerous attacks which were primarily aimed at Iraqi administrators. The group launched attacks on voters during the Iraqi legislative election in January, a combined suicide and conventional attack on the Abu Ghraib prison in April, and coordinated suicide attacks outside the Sheraton Ishtar and Palestine Hotel in Baghdad in October. In July, AQI claimed responsibility for the kidnapping and execution of Ihab Al-Sherif, Egypt's envoy to Iraq. Also in July, a three-day series of suicide attacks, including the Musayyib marketplace bombing, left at least 150 people dead. Al-Zarqawi claimed responsibility for a single-day series of more than a dozen bombings in Baghdad in September, including a bomb attack on 14 September which killed about 160 people, most of whom were unemployed Shia workers. They claimed responsibility for a series of mosque bombings in the same month in the city of Khanaqin, which killed at least 74 people.

The attacks blamed on or claimed by AQI continued to increase in 2006. In one of the incidents, two US soldiers—Thomas Lowell Tucker and Kristian Menchaca—were captured, tortured and beheaded by the ISI. In another, four Russian embassy officials were abducted and subsequently killed. Iraq's al-Qaeda and its umbrella groups were blamed for multiple attacks targeting the country's Shia population, some of which AQI claimed responsibility for.

The US claimed without verification that the group was at least one of the forces behind the wave of chlorine bombings in Iraq, which affected hundreds of people, albeit with few fatalities, after a series of crude chemical warfare attacks between late 2006 and mid 2007. During 2006, several key members of AQI were killed or captured by American and allied forces. This included al-Zarqawi himself, killed on 7 June 2006, his spiritual adviser Sheik Abd-Al-Rahman, and the alleged "number two" deputy leader, Hamid Juma Faris Jouri al-Saeedi. The group's leadership was then assumed by a man called Abu Hamza al-Muhajir, who in reality was the Egyptian militant Abu Ayyub al-Masri.

Inciting Sectarian Violence

Attacks against militiamen often targeted the Iraqi Shia majority in an attempt to incite sectarian violence. Al-Zarqawi purportedly declared an all-out war on Shias while claiming responsibility for the Shia mosque bombings. The same month, a letter allegedly written by al-Zawahiri—later rejected as a "fake" by the AQI—appeared to question the insurgents' tactic of indiscriminately attacking Shias in Iraq. In a video that appeared in December 2007, al-Zawahiri defended the AQI, but distanced himself from the crimes against civilians committed by "hypocrites and traitors" that he said existed among its ranks.

US and Iraqi officials accused the AQI of trying to slide Iraq into a full-scale civil war between Iraq's majority Shia and minority Sunni Arabs via an orchestrated campaign of militiamen massacres and a number of provocative attacks against high-profile religious targets. With attacks purportedly mounted by the AQI such as the Imam Ali Mosque bombing in 2003, the Day of Ashura bombings and Karbala and Najaf bombings in 2004, the first al-Askari Mosque bombing in Samarra in 2006, the deadly single-day series of bombings in November 2006 in which at least 215 people were killed in Baghdad's Shia district of Sadr City, and the second al-Askari bombing in 2007, the AQI provoked Shia militias to unleash a wave of retaliatory attacks. The result was a plague of death squad-style killings and a spiral into further sectarian violence, which escalated in 2006 and brought Iraq to the brink of violent anarchy in 2007. In 2008, sectarian bombings blamed on al-Qaeda killed at least 42 people at the Imam Husayn Shrine in Karbala in March and at least 51 people at a bus stop in Baghdad in June.

Operations Outside Iraq and Other Activities

On 3 December 2004, AQI attempted to blow up an Iraqi–Jordanian border crossing, but failed to do so. In 2006, a Jordanian court sentenced to death al-Zarqawi *in absentia* and two of his associates for their involvement in the plot. AQI increased its presence outside Iraq by claiming credit for three attacks in 2005.

In the most deadly of these attacks, suicide bombs killed 60 people in Amman, Jordan on 9 November 2005. They claimed responsibility for the rocket attacks that narrowly missed the USS *Kearsarge* and USS *Ashland* in Jordan, which also targeted the city of Eilat in Israel, and for the firing of several rockets into Israel from Lebanon in December 2005.

The Lebanese-Palestinian militant group Fatah al-Islam, which was defeated by Lebanese government forces during the 2007 Lebanon conflict, was linked to AQI and led by al-Zarqawi's former companion who had fought alongside him in Iraq. The group may have been linked to the little-known group called "Tawhid and Jihad in Syria", and may have influenced the Palestinian resistance group in Gaza called "Tawhid and Jihad Brigades", better known as the Army of Islam.

American officials believed that Al-Qaeda in Iraq had conducted bomb attacks against Syrian government forces. Al-Nusra Front, another al-Qaeda-inspired group, claimed responsibility for attacks inside Syria, and Iraqi Foreign Minister Hoshyar Zebari said that Al-Qaeda in Iraq members were going to Syria, where the militants had previously received support and weapons.

Goals and Umbrella Organizations

In a letter to Ayman al-Zawahiri in July 2005, al-Zarqawi outlined a four-stage plan to expand the Iraq War, which included expelling US forces from Iraq, establishing an Islamic authority—a caliphate—spreading the conflict to Iraq's secular neighbors, and engaging in the Arab–Israeli conflict. The affiliated groups were linked to regional attacks outside Iraq which were consistent with their stated plan, one example being the 2005 Sharm al-Sheikh bombings in Egypt, which killed 88 people, many of them foreign tourists.

In January 2006, Al-Qaeda in Iraq (AQI)—the name by which *Tanzim Qaidat al-Jihad fi Bilad al-Rafidayn* was more commonly known—created an umbrella organization called the Mujahideen Shura Council (MSC), in an attempt to unify Sunni insurgents in Iraq. Its efforts to recruit Iraqi Sunni nationalists and secular groups were undermined by the violent tactics it used against civilians and its extreme Islamic fundamentalist doctrine. Because of these impediments, the attempt was largely unsuccessful.

AQI attributed its attacks to the MSC until mid-October 2006, when Abu Ayyub al-Masri declared the formation of the self-styled Islamic State of Iraq (ISI). This was another front which included the Shura Council factions. AQI then began attributing its attacks to the ISI. According to a study compiled by US intelligence agencies, the ISI had plans to seize power and turn the country into a Sunni Islamic state.

AS ISLAMIC STATE OF IRAQ (2006–2013)

Strength and Activity

In 2006, the State Department's Bureau of Intelligence and Research estimated that Al-Qaeda in Iraq's core membership was "more than 1,000". These figures do not include the other six AQI-led Salafi groups in the Islamic State of Iraq. In 2007 estimates of the group's strength ranged from just 850 to several thousand full-time fighters. The group was said to be suffering high manpower losses, including those from its many "martyrdom" operations, but for a long time this appeared to have little effect on its strength and capabilities, implying a constant flow of volunteers from Iraq and abroad. However, Al-Qaeda in Iraq more than doubled in strength, from 1,000 to 2,500 fighters, after the US withdrawal from Iraq in late 2011.

In 2007, some observers and scholars suggested that the threat posed by AQI was being exaggerated and that a "heavy focus on al-Qaeda obscures a much more complicated situation on the ground". According to the July 2007 National Intelligence Estimate and the Defense Intelligence Agency reports, AQI accounted for 15% percent of attacks in Iraq. However, the Congressional Research Service noted in its September 2007 report that attacks from al-Qaeda were less than 2% of the violence in Iraq. It criticized the Bush administration's statistics, noting that its false reporting of insurgency attacks as AQI attacks had increased since the surge operations began in 2007. In March 2007, the US-sponsored Radio

Free Europe/Radio Liberty analysed AQI attacks for that month and concluded that the group had taken credit for 43 out of 439 attacks on Iraqi security forces and Shia militias, and 17 out of 357 attacks on US troops.

According to the 2006 US Government report, this group was most clearly associated with foreign jihadist cells operating in Iraq and had specifically targeted international forces and Iraqi citizens; most of Al-Qaeda in Iraq (AQI)'s operatives were not Iraqi, but were coming through a series of safe houses, the largest of which was on the Iraq-Syrian border. AQI's operations were predominately Iraq-based, but the United States Department of State alleged that the group maintained an extensive logistical network throughout the Middle East, North Africa, South Asia and Europe. In a June 2008 CNN special report, Al-Qaeda in Iraq was called "a well-oiled... organization... almost as pedantically bureaucratic as was Saddam Hussein's Ba'ath Party", collecting new execution videos long after they stopped publicising them, and having a network of spies even in the US military bases. According to the report, Iraqis—many of them former members of Hussein's secret services—were now effectively running Al-Qaeda in Iraq, with "foreign fighters' roles" seeming to be "mostly relegated to the cannon fodder of suicide attacks", although the organization's top leadership was still dominated by non-Iraqis.

Decline

The high-profile attacks linked to the group continued through early 2007, as AQI claimed responsibility for attacks such as the March assassination attempt on Sunni Deputy Prime Minister of Iraq Salam al-Zaubai, the April Iraqi Parliament bombing, and the May capture and subsequent execution of three American soldiers. Also in May, ISI leader al-Baghdadi was declared to have been killed in Baghdad, but his death was later denied by the insurgents; later, al-Baghdadi was even declared by the US to be non-existent. There were conflicting reports regarding the fate of al-Masri. From March to August, coalition forces fought the Battle of Baqubah as part of the largely successful attempts to wrest the Diyala Governorate from AQI-aligned forces. Through 2007, the majority of suicide bombings targeting civilians in Iraq were routinely identified by military and government sources as being the responsibility of al-Qaeda and its associated groups, even when there was no claim of responsibility, as was the case in the 2007 Yazidi communities bombings, which killed some 800 people in the deadliest terrorist attack in Iraq to date.

By late 2007, violent and indiscriminate attacks directed by rogue AQI elements against Iraqi civilians had severely damaged their image and caused loss of support among the population, thus isolating the group. In a major blow to AQI, many former Sunni militants who had previously fought alongside the group started to work with the American forces. The US troops surge supplied the military with more manpower for operations targeting the group, resulting in dozens of high-level AQI members being captured or killed. Al-Qaeda seemed to have lost its foothold in Iraq and appeared to be severely crippled. Accordingly, the bounty issued for al-Masri was eventually cut from $5 million to $100,000 in April 2008.

As of 2008, a series of US and Iraqi offensives managed to drive out the AQI-aligned insurgents from their former safe havens, such as the Diyala and Al Anbar governorates and the embattled capital of Baghdad, to the area of the northern city of Mosul, the latest of the Iraq War's major battlegrounds. The struggle for control of Ninawa Governorate—the Ninawa campaign—was launched in January 2008 by US and Iraqi forces as part of the large-scale Operation Phantom Phoenix, which was aimed at combating al-Qaeda activity in and around Mosul, and finishing off the network's remnants in central Iraq that had escaped Operation Phantom Thunder in 2007. In Baghdad a pet market was bombed in February 2008 and a shopping centre was bombed in March 2008, killing at least 98 and 68 people respectively; AQI were the suspected perpetrators.

AQI has long raised money, running into tens of millions of dollars, from kidnappings for ransom, car theft—sometimes killing drivers in the process—hijacking fuel trucks and other activities. According to an April 2007 statement by their Islamic Army in Iraq rivals, AQI was demanding *jizya* tax and killing members of wealthy families when it was not paid. According to both US and

Iraqi sources, in May 2008 AQI was stepping up its fundraising campaigns as its strictly militant capabilities were on the wane, with especially lucrative activity said to be oil operations centered on the industrial city of Bayji. According to US military intelligence sources, in 2008 the group resembled a "Mafia-esque criminal gang".

Conflicts with other Groups

The first reports of a split and even armed clashes between Al-Qaeda in Iraq and other Sunni groups date back to 2005. In the summer of 2006, local Sunni tribes and insurgent groups, including the prominent Islamist-nationalist group Islamic Army in Iraq (IAI), began to speak of their dissatisfaction with al-Qaeda and its tactics, openly criticizing the foreign fighters for their deliberate targeting of Iraqi civilians. In September 2006, 30 Anbar tribes formed their own local alliance called the Anbar Salvation Council (ASC), which was directed specifically at countering al-Qaeda-allied terrorist forces in the province, and they openly sided with the government and the US troops.

By the beginning of 2007, Sunni tribes and nationalist insurgents had begun battling with their former allies in AQI in order to retake control of their communities. In early 2007, forces allied to Al-Qaeda in Iraq committed a series of attacks on Sunnis critical of the group, including the February 2007 attack in which scores of people were killed when a truck bomb exploded near a Sunni mosque in Fallujah. Al-Qaeda supposedly played a role in the assassination of the leader of the Anbar-based insurgent group 1920 Revolution Brigade, the military wing of the Islamic Resistance Movement. In April 2007, the IAI spokesman accused the ISI of killing at least 30 members of the IAI, as well as members of the Jamaat Ansar al-Sunna and Mujahideen Army insurgent groups, and called on Osama bin Laden to intervene personally to rein in Al-Qaeda in Iraq.

The following month, the government announced that AQI leader al-Masri had been killed by ASC fighters. Four days later, AQI released an audio tape in which a man claiming to be al-Masri warned Sunnis not to take part in the political process; he also said that reports of internal fighting between Sunni militia groups were "lies and fabrications". Later in May, the US forces announced the release of dozens of Iraqis who were tortured by AQI as a part of the group's intimidation campaign.

By June 2007, the growing hostility between foreign-influenced jihadists and Sunni nationalists had led to open gun battles between the groups in Baghdad. The Islamic Army soon reached a ceasefire agreement with AQI, but refused to sign on to the ISI.

There were reports that Hamas of Iraq insurgents were involved in assisting US troops in their Diyala Governorate operations against Al-Qaeda in August 2007. In September 2007, AQI claimed responsibility for the assassination of three people including the prominent Sunni sheikh Abdul Sattar Abu Risha, leader of the Anbar "Awakening council". That same month, a suicide attack on a mosque in the city of Baqubah killed 28 people, including members of Hamas of Iraq and the 1920 Revolution Brigade, during a meeting at the mosque between tribal and guerilla leaders and the police. Meanwhile, the US military began arming moderate insurgent factions when they promised to fight Al-Qaeda in Iraq instead of the Americans.

By December 2007, the strength of the "Awakening" movement irregulars—also called "Concerned Local Citizens" and "Sons of Iraq"—was estimated at 65,000–80,000 fighters. Many of them were former insurgents, including alienated former AQI supporters, and they were now being armed and paid by the Americans specifically to combat al-Qaeda's presence in Iraq. As of July 2007, this highly controversial strategy proved to be effective in helping to secure the Sunni districts of Baghdad and the other hotspots of central Iraq, and to root out the al-Qaeda-aligned militants.

By 2008, the ISI was describing itself as being in a state of "extraordinary crisis", which was attributable to a number of factors, notably the Anbar Awakening.

Transformation and Resurgence

In early 2009, US forces began pulling out of cities across the country, turning over the task of maintaining security to the Iraqi Army, the Iraqi Police Service and their paramilitary allies. Experts and many Iraqis were worried that in the absence of US soldiers the ISI might resurface and attempt mass-casualty attacks to destabilize the country. There was indeed a spike in the number of suicide attacks, and through mid- and late 2009, the ISI rebounded in strength and appeared to be launching a concerted effort to cripple the Iraqi government. During August and October 2009, the ISI claimed responsibility for four bombings targeting five government buildings in Baghdad, including attacks that killed 101 at the ministries of Foreign Affairs and Finance in August and 155 at the Ministry of Justice and Ministry of Municipalities and Public Works in September; these were the deadliest attacks directed at the new government in more than six years of war. These attacks represented a shift away from the group's previous efforts to incite sectarian violence, although a series of suicide attacks in April targeted mainly Iranian Shia pilgrims, killing 76, and in June, a mosque bombing in Taza killed at least 73 Shias from the Turkmen ethnic minority.

In late 2009, the commander of the US forces in Iraq, General Ray Odierno, stated that the ISI "has transformed significantly in the last two years. What once was dominated by foreign individuals has now become more and more dominated by Iraqi citizens". Odierno's comments reinforced accusations by the government of Nouri al-Maliki that al-Qaeda and ex-Ba'athists were working together to undermine improved security and sabotage the planned Iraqi parliamentary elections in 2010. On 18 April 2010, the ISI's two top leaders, Abu Ayyub al-Masri and Abu Omar al-Baghdadi, were killed in a joint US-Iraqi raid near Tikrit. In a press conference in June 2010, General Odierno reported that 80% of the ISI's top 42 leaders, including recruiters and financiers, had been killed or captured, with only eight remaining at large. He said that they had been cut off from Al Qaeda's leadership in Pakistan, and that improved intelligence had enabled the successful mission in April that led to the killing of al-Masri and al-Baghdadi; in addition, the number of attacks and casualty figures in Iraq for the first five months of 2010 were the lowest since 2003. In May 2011, the Islamic State of Iraq's "emir of Baghdad" Huthaifa al-Batawi, captured during the crackdown after the 2010 Baghdad church attack in which 68 people died, was killed during an attempted prison break, during which an Iraqi general and several others were also killed.

On 16 May 2010, Abu Bakr al-Baghdadi was appointed the new leader of the Islamic State of Iraq; he had previously been the general supervisor of the group's provincialsharia committees and a member of its senior consultative council. Al-Baghdadi replenished the group's leadership, many of whom had been killed or captured, by appointing former Ba'athist military and intelligence officers who had served during the Saddam Hussein regime. These men, nearly all of whom had spent time imprisoned by American forces, came to make up about one-third of Baghdadi's top 25 commanders. One of them was a former Colonel, Samir al-Khlifawi, also known as Haji Bakr, who became the overall military commander in charge of overseeing the group's operations.

In July 2012, al-Baghdadi's first audio statement was released online. In this he announced that the group was returning to the former strongholds that US troops and their Sunni allies had driven them from prior to the withdrawal of US troops. He also declared the start of a new offensive in Iraq called *Breaking the Walls* which would focus on freeing members of the group held in Iraqi prisons. Violence in Iraq began to escalate that month, and in the following year the group carried out 24 waves of VBIED attacks and eight prison breaks. By July 2013, monthly fatalities had exceeded 1,000 for the first time since April 2008. The *Breaking the Walls* campaign culminated in July 2013, with the group carrying out simultaneous raids on Taji and Abu Ghraib prison, freeing more than 500 prisoners, many of them veterans of the Iraqi insurgency.

Abu Bakr al-Baghdadi was declared a Specially Designated Global Terrorist on 4 October 2011 by the US State Department, with an announced reward of US$10 million for information leading to his capture or death.

AS ISLAMIC STATE OF IRAQ AND THE LEVANT (2013–2014)

Declaration and Dispute with al-Nusra Front

In March 2011, protests began in Syria against the government of Bashar al-Assad. In the following month violence between demonstrators and security forces led to a gradual militarisation of thc conflict. In August 2011, Abu Bakr al-Baghdadi began sending Syrian and Iraqi ISI members, experienced in guerilla warfare, across the border into Syria to establish an organization inside the country. Led by a Syrian known as Abu Muhammad al-Jawlani, the group began to recruit fighters and establish cells throughout the country. On 23 January 2012, the group announced its formation as *Jabhat al-Nusra l'Ahl as-Sham*—Jabhat al-Nusra—more commonly known as al-Nusra Front. Al-Nusra rapidly expanded into a capable fighting force with a level of popular support among opposition supporters in Syria.

In April 2013, al-Baghdadi released an audio statement in which he announced that al-Nusra Front had been established, financed and supported by the Islamic State of Iraq and that the two groups were merging under the name "Islamic State of Iraq and Al-Sham". Al-Jawlani issued a statement denying the merger and complaining that neither he nor anyone else in al-Nusra's leadership had been consulted about it. In June 2013, Al Jazeera reported that it had obtained a letter written by al-Qaedaleader Ayman al-Zawahiri, addressed to both leaders, in which he ruled against the merger and appointed an emissary to oversee relations between them and put an end to tensions. In the same month, al-Baghdadi released an audio message rejecting al-Zawahiri's ruling and declaring that the merger was going ahead. In October 2013, al-Zawahiri ordered the disbanding of ISIS, putting al-Nusra Front in charge of jihadist efforts in Syria, but al-Baghdadi contested al-Zawahiri's ruling on the basis of Islamic jurisprudence and the group continued to operate in Syria. In February 2014, after an eight-month power struggle, al-Qaeda disavowed any relations with ISIS.

According to journalist Sarah Birke, there are "significant differences" between al-Nusra Front and ISIS. While al-Nusra actively calls for the overthrow of the Assad government, ISIS "tends to be more focused on establishing its own rule on conquered territory". ISIS is "far more ruthless" in building an Islamic state, "carrying out sectarian attacks and imposing sharia law immediately", she said. While al-Nusra has a "large contingent of foreign fighters", it is seen as a home-grown group by many Syrians; by contrast, ISIS fighters have been described as "foreign 'occupiers'" by many Syrian refugees. It has a strong presence in mid- and northern Syria, where it has instituted sharia in a number of towns. The group reportedly controlled the four border towns of Atmeh, al-Bab, Azaz and Jarablus, allowing it to control the exit and entrance from Syria into Turkey. Foreign fighters in Syria include Russian-speaking jihadists who were part of Jaish al-Muhajireen wal-Ansar (JMA). In November 2013, the JMA's ethnic Chechen leader Abu Omar al-Shishani swore an oath of allegiance to al-Baghdadi; the group then split between those who followed al-Shishani in joining ISIS and those who continued to operate independently in the JMA under a new leadership.

In May 2014, al-Qaeda leader Ayman al-Zawahiri ordered al-Nusra Front to stop attacks on its rival ISIS. In June 2014, after continued fighting between the two groups, al-Nusra's branch in the Syrian town of al-Bukamal pledged allegiance to ISIS.

Conflicts with other Groups

In Syria, rebels affiliated with the Islamic Front and the Free Syrian Army launched an offensive against ISIS militants in and around Aleppo in January 2014.

Suggested Ties with the Syrian Government

In January 2014, *The Daily Telegraph* said that Western "intelligence sources" believed that the Syrian government made secret oil deals with ISIS and al-Nusra Front, alleging that the militants were funding their campaign by selling crude oil to the regime from the fields they have captured.

AS *ISLAMIC STATE* (2014–PRESENT)

On 29 June 2014, ISIS removed "Iraq and the Levant" from its name and began to refer to itself as the Islamic State, declaring the territory under its control a new caliphate and naming Abu Bakr al-Baghdadi as its caliph.

On the first night of Ramadan, Shaykh Abu Muhammad al-Adnani al-Shami, spokesperson for ISIS, described the establishment of the caliphate as "a dream that lives in the depths of every Muslim believer" and "the abandoned obligation of the era". He said that the group's ruling Shura Council had decided to establish the caliphate formally and that Muslims around the world should now pledge their allegiance to the new caliph. The declaration of a caliphate has been criticized and ridiculed by Muslim scholars and rival Islamists inside and outside the occupied territory.

Analysts observed that dropping the reference to region reflected a widening of the group's scope, and Laith Alkhouri, a terrorism analyst, thought that after capturing many areas in Syria and Iraq, ISIS felt this was a suitable opportunity to take control of the global jihadist movement. A week before its change of name to the Islamic State, ISIS had captured the Trabil crossing on the Jordan–Iraq border, the only border crossing between the two countries.

ISIS has received some public support in Jordan, albeit limited, partly owing to state repression there. Raghad Hussein, the daughter of Saddam Hussein now living in opulent asylum in Jordan, has publicly expressed support for the advance of ISIS in Iraq, reflecting the Ba'athist alliance of convenience with ISIS with the goal of return to power in Bagdad.

ISIS undertook a recruitment drive in Saudi Arabia, where tribes in the north are linked to those in western Iraq and eastern Syria.

In June and July 2014, Jordan and Saudi Arabia moved troops to their borders with Iraq after Iraq lost control of, or withdrew from, strategic crossing points, which were thence under ISIS's command. There was speculation that al-Maliki had ordered a withdrawal of troops from the Iraq–Saudi crossings in order "to increase pressure on Saudi Arabia and bring the threat of ISIS over-running its borders as well". After the group captured Kurdish-controlled territory and massacred Yazidis, the US launched a humanitarian mission and aerial bombing campaign against ISIS.

In July 2014, Boko Haram leader Abubakar Shekau declared support for the new Calpihate and Caliph Ibrahim. In August,

Abubakar Shekau announced that Boko Haram had captured the Nigerian town of Gwoza in the name of the Caliphate. Shekau announced: "Thanks be to Allah who gave victory to our brothers in Gwoza and made it part of the Islamic caliphate". This announcement appears to be unilateral.

The moderate rebels in the Free Syrian Army had been backed by the United States with weapons and training, but in August 2014, a high-level commander in the Islamic State stated: "In the East of Syria, there is no Free Syrian Army any longer. All Free Syrian Army people [there] have joined the Islamic State". The Islamic State recruited more than 6,300 fighters in July 2014 alone, many of them coming from the Free Syrian Army.

Human Rights Abuses

ISIS compels people in the areas it controls, under the penalty of death, torture or mutilation, to declare Islamic creed, and live according to its interpretation of Sunni Islamand sharia law. It directs violence against Shia Muslims, indigenous Assyrian, Chaldean, Syriac and Armenian Christians, Yazidis, Druze, Shabaks and Mandeans in particular.

Treatment of Civilians

During the Iraqi conflict in 2014, ISIS released dozens of videos showing its ill treatment of civilians, many of whom had apparently been targeted on the basis of their religion or ethnicity. Navi Pillay, UN High Commissioner for Human Rights, warned of war crimes occurring in the Iraqi war zone, and disclosed one UN report of ISIS militants murdering Iraqi Army soldiers and 17 civilians in a single street in Mosul. The United Nations reported that in the 17 days from 5 to 22 June, ISIS killed more than 1,000 Iraqi civilians and injured more than 1,000. After ISIS released photographs of its fighters shooting scores of young men, the United Nations declared that cold-blooded "executions" said to have been carried out by militants in northern Iraq almost certainly amounted to war crimes.

ISIS's advance in Iraq in mid-2014 was accompanied by continuing violence in Syria. On 29 May, a village in Syria was raided by ISIS and at least 15 civilians were killed, including, according to Human Rights Watch, at least six children. A hospital in the area confirmed that it had received 15 bodies on the same day. The Syrian Observatory for Human Rights reported that on 1 June, a 102-year-old man was killed along with his whole family in a village in Hama. ISIS has recruited to its ranks Iraqi children, who can be seen with masks on their faces and guns in their hands patrolling the streets of Mosul.

Sexual Violence Allegations

According to one report, ISIS's capture of Iraqi cities in June 2014 was accompanied by an upsurge in crimes against women, including kidnap and rape. *The Guardian* reported that ISIS's extremist agenda extended to women's bodies and that women living under their control were being captured and raped. Hannaa Edwar, a leading women's rights advocate in Baghdad who runs an NGO called al-Amal, said that none of her contacts in Mosul were able to confirm any cases of rape; however, another Baghdad-based women's rights activist, Basma al-Khateeb, said that a culture of violence existed in Iraq against women generally and felt sure that sexual violence against women was happening in Mosul involving not only ISIS but all armed groups. During a meeting with Nouri al-Maliki, Cyprus British Foreign Minister William Hague said with regard to ISIS: "Anyone glorifying, supporting or joining it should understand that they would be assisting a group responsible for kidnapping, torture, executions, rape and many other hideous crimes". According to Martin Williams in *The Citizen,* some hard-line Salafists apparently regard extramarital sex with multiple partners as a legitimate form of holy war and it is "difficult to reconcile this with a religion where some adherents insist that women must be covered from head to toe, with only a narrow slit for the eyes". Yezidi girls in Iraq were allegedly raped by ISIS fighters and subsequently committed suicide, as described in a witness statement recorded by Rudaw.

Guidelines for Civilians

After the self-proclaimed Islamic State captured cities in Iraq, ISIS issued guidelines on how to wear clothes and veils. ISIS warned women in the city of Mosul to wear full-face veils or face severe punishment. A cleric told Reuters in Mosul that ISIS gunmen had ordered him to read out the warning in his mosque when worshippers gathered. ISIS also banned naked mannequins and ordered the faces of both male and female mannequins to be covered. ISIS released 16 notes labeled "Contract of the City", a set of rules aimed at civilians in Nineveh. One rule stipulated that women should stay at home and not go outside unless necessary. Another rule said that stealing would be punished by amputation.

Christians living in areas under ISIS control who wanted to remain in the "caliphate" faced three options: converting to Islam, paying a religious levy—jizya—or death. "We offer them three choices: Islam; the dhimma contract – involving payment of jizya; if they refuse this they will have nothing but the sword", ISIS said. ISIS had already set similar rules for Christians in Ar-Raqqah, Syria, once one of the nation's most liberal cities.

3

Terrorism Groups of Islamic State in Iraq and Syria (ISIS)

The Islamic State of Iraq and the Levant [ISIL] declared itself an "Islamic caliphate" on 29 June 2014, led by Caliph Ibrahim. This came as many of the world's estimated 1.6 billion Muslims started observing the holy month of Ramadan. ISIL spokesman Abu Muhammad al-Adnani said the caliphate will extend from the northern Syrian city of Aleppo to Diyala Province in Iraq. He described the establishment of the caliphate as "the dream in all the Muslims" and "the hope of all jihadists." They removed 'Iraq and the Levant' from their name and urged other radical Sunni groups to pledge their allegiance. ISIL announced that it should now be called 'The Islamic State' and declared its chief, Abu Bakr al-Baghdadi, as "the caliph" of the new state and "leader for Muslims everywhere," the radical Sunni militant group said in an audio recording distributed online on Sunday. This is the first time since the fall of the Ottoman Empire in 1923 that a Caliph – which meant a political successor to Prophet Muhammad – had been declared.

The State Department's Deputy Assistant Secretary of State for Iraq and Iran, Brett McGurk, described ISIL as "a full-blown army" and "worse than al-Qaida" - with a potential reach far beyond the Middle East. In testimony on 24 July 2014 he said "ISIL is able to funnel 30 to 50 suicide bombers a month into Iraq. We assess these are almost all foreign fighters" he said. "It would be very easy for ISIL to decide to funnel that cadre of dedicated suicide bombers

- global jihadists - into other capitals around the region, or Europe, or, worse, here [in the United States]."

The Islamic State of Iraq and the Levant [ISIL] or "Greater Syria", which translates to "al-Sham" (ISIS) [Da'esh is the Arabic equivalent of the acronym ISIS], aims to establish an Islamic state in the regions it controls in eastern Syria and western Iraq. It aims to control at least the Sunni part of Iraq, and much of Syria and Lebanon. The emergence of a radical jihadist state in the heart of the Arab world would threaten the US, and American allies in the Middle East and Europe. In the long term the Islamic State in Iraq and the Levant wants to be a global power, and, with the resources it is acquiring, the West and its allies face a difficult job to stop it.

There are signs it was backed by former military officers and other members of Saddam Hussein's regime — including the Naqshabandi Army led by Izzat Ibrahim al-Douri, the former regime's number two leader who eluded US and Iraqi forces ever since the 2003 US-led invasion. The reinvigorated Ba'athist Party, known as the Jaysh Rijal al-Tariqah al-Naqshabandia (JRTN), clings to Baathist ideology and often mix it with Islamic sufi ideology. JRTN and the ISIL worked together in Fallujah, where they have been battling government troops since January 2014. In conjunction with ISIL they were able to take Mosul. Overwhelmingly a majority of the fighters under the ISIL banner are Iraqi.

ISIL continued to gain strength from the struggle in Syria resulting in an overflow of recruits, sophisticated munitions and other resources to the fight in Iraq. The threat that ISIL is presenting is not just a threat to Iraq or the stability of Iraq, but it is a threat to the region.

The states of Iraq and Syria are not able to control major population centers and have lost control of huge countryside areas. This meant that ISIL control territory, border crossing points, oil resources, mineral resources, and TRADE income. They have a base in the middle of the Middle East, and can organize and carry out their goals in larger parts of the Middle East.

A statement attributed to Al-Qaida posted 03 February 2014 on websites frequently used by al-Qaida announced it was severing ties with the Islamic State of Iraq and the Levant, or ISIL [the authenticity of the statement could not be independently verified]. The move was seen as an attempt to redirect the Islamist effort towards unseating President Bashar al-Assad rather than waste resources in fighting other rebels. ISIL has fought battles with other Islamist insurgents and secular rebel groups, often triggered by disputes over authority and territory. Several secular and Islamist groups announced a campaign in January 2014 against ISIL.

Black-clad al-Qaida militants in Iraq seized control of the embattled western city of Fallujah on January 03, 2014, raising their flag over government buildings and declaring an independent Islamic state. Witnesses said the Sunni militants, members of the Islamic State of Iraq and al-Sham, or ISIS, cut power lines in the city late in the day and ordered residents not to use backup generators. But the chief of Fallujah police, Mohamed al-Isawi, disputed the ISIS claims of control, telling The New York Times newspaper that he was repositioning his forces north of the city for a decisive battle. He said his personnel had been strengthened by an alliance of tribal leaders. The Iraqi Army repeatedly attacked and shelled the towns of Ramadi and Falluja for months thereafter, failing for the most part to dislodge the militants.

The militants' seizure of Iraqi cities in June 2014 and their swift advance southward constitute a stunning defeat for the country's Shi'ite-led government. Hundreds of fleeing soldiers reportedly tore off their uniforms and fled their posts for the safety of nearby Kurdistan. The Iraqi government called June 10, 2014 for parliament to declare a state of emergency, after militants from the al Qaida-affiliated "Islamic State of Iraq and the Levant" seized control of most of the northern city of Mosul and Nineveh Province. Islamic militants captured police and army positions, setting fire to vehicles. Militants also seized the airport, government offices and banks. Gunbattles between the militants and the army raged for hours, before the Iraqi military finally withdrew to positions north of the city.

Sunni Parliament Speaker Osama al Nujeifi, a political adversary of Maliki, accused the Iraqi military of abandoning Mosul, as well as their equipment, weapons and ammunition, to the Islamic militants. He said that the Mosul governor's office warned army leaders in recent weeks about the presence of armed militants in the region, but they took no preventive measures, so that when the battle came to the city, they laid down their weapons, and fled, leaving everything to the terrorists. The parliament speaker's brother is the provincial governor of Mosul and surrounding Ninevah Province.

Militants from the Islamic State in Iraq and the Levant overran the city of Tikrit and closed in on Iraq's biggest OIL refinery in the town of Beiji, a day after seizing Iraq's second-largest city, Mosul. By late 11 June 2014, militants had reached the edge of Samarra, an important Shi'ite shrine almost 113 kilometers, or 70 miles, north of Baghdad. The militants threatened to destroy the shrine unless government forces left.

Sunni jihadists prepared for an assault on Samarra, home to a revered Al-Askari Shia shrine, a terror attack on which back in 2006 already sparked a sectarian war in Iraq. The militants had already tried to capture Samarra, 110km from the capital, Baghdad, twice over the last two weeks. The local tribal security forces have turned down the proposal of the militants to leave peacefully though militants promised not to destroy the shrine. A bomb explosion in 2006 resulted in mass fighting throughout the country and the deaths of tens of thousands of people.

Hawkish Republican Lindsey Graham (Republican-South Carolina) said 13 June 2014 " I'm not the commander in chief. I'm tired of telling him what to do. It's not really my place to tell him what to do... The people in the ISIS [Islamic State in Iraq and Greater Syria, and/or the Levant] have as part of their agenda to attack our homeland. The next 9/11 is in the making. Syria has become the Afghanistan before 9/11 — it's a place for safe havens and training."

ISIL claimed to have executed 1,700 Shi'ite recruits in Tikrit and posted photos online showing dead bodies purportedly belonging to those executed. An Iraqi military spokesman, Qassim al-Mussawi, confirmed the authenticity of the photos, saying that analysis shows at least 170 slain recruits were shown in the brutal images.

When ISIS took control of Mosul in the northwest of the country, militants presented Christians with the traditional ultimatum from the time of the Prophet. They were given a choice of converting to Islam, paying the tax for non-Muslims, leaving their homes, or being put to the sword. After the given deadline, militants started violent actions and hundreds of Christian families fled their homes. While some families chose to stay and pay the tax, those who fled were sometimes stopped at checkpoints by militants and had their MONEY, jewellery, mobile phones and medicine confiscated.

The Organization of Islamic Cooperation (OIC) on 21 July 2014 condemned ISIL for what it called the "forced deportation" of Christians under the threat of execution, "thus further tearing apart the social fabric of the Iraqi people." OIC Secretary-General Iyad Ameen Madani condemned what he called "the terrorist group" and said such atrocities contradict the principles of the OIC "that call for the entrenchment of a culture of tolerance and affinity among all nations and peoples."

In June 2014, the Islamic State in Iraq and the Levant (ISIL) reportedly seized control of nuclear material controlled by the Iraqi government at the University of Mosul. The ISIL also entered the al-Muthanna project site located 60 miles north of Baghdad near the town of Samarra where the "remnants of the former [Iraqi] chemical weapons program were kept." During the 1980s, the site produced hundreds of tons of Sarin, VX, and mustard agents. Aerial bombing during Desert Storm destroyed the research and production facilities at al-Muthanna and ended its ability to produce chemical weapons. The exact contents of the two bunkers that the ISIL entered, however, are not generally known. The lack of control of radioactive materials and former chemical weapons agents in Iraq is a concern, but the requisites to make the stolen materials into a weapon of mass destruction were lacking.

The Islamic State group (IS) executed 700 people from a Syrian tribe it had been battling in eastern Syria over the past two weeks, the majority of whom were civilians, a Syrian monitoring group said 16 August 2014. The British-based Syrian Observatory for Human Rights, which has consistently tracked violence on both sides of the three-year-old Syrian civil war have said that around 700 members of the al-Sheitaat tribe, from the Deir al-Zor province, had been executed and that many of them were beheaded by IS jihadists.

Funding and Strength

The sources and extent of ISIL's FUNDING and power remain unclear. It is apparent that this organization has been well-funded for years. After raiding Mosul's central bank and stealing an estimated $429 million in June 2014, one report speculated that the ISIL may now be sitting on nearly $1.5 billion in assets.[Current reporting suggested that the ISIL continued to pay competitive salaries and death benefits to its members in a more reliable fashion than the Iraqi Army.

Iraqi Prime Minister Nuri al-Maliki's office on 17 June 2014 issued a statement accusing Saudi Arabia of giving ISIL "financial and moral support." State FUNDING by Saudi Arabia was complicated to prove but private giving was not. There were many private donations coming out of Saudi Arabia and other Gulf states. In more recent times, ISIL had its own source of funding controlling gas and OIL fields in the east of Syria that gave it a revenue stream. And having overrun Mosul and other Iraqi cities, it acquired a lot of cash and gold bullion and military hardware.

In their fight the Syrian government, they took over some Syrian oil facilities, potentially a huge source of revenue. But they could only find one customer - Syria. By June 2013 ISIS had been selling smuggled Syrian oil in Turkey worth $800 million, according to Ali Ediboglu, a lawmaker for the border province of Hatay from the main opposition Republican People's Party (CHP). It also secured revenue by selling electricity to the Syrian government from captured power plants. The militants set their sights on Iraq's Beiji oil facility, potentially providing another source of revenue to further expand their operations.

Iraq lost approximately four divisions worth of equipment and probably at least three depots in the area of Mosul. Much of the equipment taken by the Islamic State when the Iraqi army fled Mosul was front-line American weaponry. Multiple reports said the loot included US Stinger surface-to-air missiles, artillery pieces, Humvees, and heavy trucks, not to mention piles of assault rifles and ammunition. Some of this would be usable, but much of it would not, in the absence of training and spare parts for maintenance.

ISIS led a coalition of Sunni militias in an astonishing takeover of a considerable portion of the Iraq's northern oil fields. The group has begun to smuggle close to $1 million per day in Iraqi crude, prompting some to dub the insurgents' still-fragile Islamic caliphate "the world's smallest petro-state."

While the Pentagon said it was hard to put a number on just how large the ISIL force is, some believed it to have 5,000 to 7,000 fighters. Other analysts said in June 2014 that between Iraq and Syria, there could be as many as 12,000 to 15,000 fighters moving across an area largely under their control, 3,000 of whom were from Western countries.

ISIS had a falling out with the Syrian Sunni radical group Jabhat al-Nusra – the Nusra Front, and the rift caused al-Qaida leader Ayman Zawahiri to disown ISIL and al-Baghdadi. But in June 2014, reports said al-Nusra agreed to send its fighters to join the Islamic State, giving its thrust into Iraq even greater energy. Many intelligence estimates have pegged al-Baghdadi's force at some 15,000. If al-Nusra, which has a similar force strength, had indeed merged there could be 30,000 fighters under the Islamic State's black banner.

Islamic State recruited at least 6,300 men in July, Rami Abdelrahman, founder of the Syrian Observatory for Human Rights, told Reuters on 19 August 2014. This was a big expansion from early estimates suggesting the group numbered around 15,000. Around a thousand of the new fighters were foreign, and the rest Syrian, he said. The surge followed Islamic State's rapid advance in northern Iraq in June, where its capture of the city of Mosul furnished it with new weaponry and resources, some of which were diverted to Syria. Much of the recruitment had taken place in Islamic State's stronghold of Raqqa.

Six years earlier, the US State Department reported that "The threat from AQI continued to diminish in 2008. AQI, although still dangerous, has experienced the defection of members, lost key mobilization areas, suffered disruption of support infrastructure and FUNDING, and been forced to change targeting priorities. Indeed, the pace of suicide bombing countryside, which we consider one indicator of AQI's operational capability, fell significantly during last year.... Membership is estimated at 2,000-4,000, making it the largest, most potent Sunni extremist group in Iraq."

In 2001, the State Department reported that "Al-Qaida may have several thousand members and associates." And in 2000 the State Department reported that Al-Qaida "May have several hundred to several thousand members."

Andreas Krieg, an expert on transnational groups in the Middle East and a lecturer at King's College London, noted in June 2014 that the Islamic State "... is quite fragile at the moment. They don't have the fighting force to actually administer the vast territory that they have gained. So I think because they are weak right now, if we act quickly, I think something can be done. But once they consolidate their power over months to come, I think we will face a much bigger problem that we will not be able to contain".

In June 2014 ISIL campaign seems to derive from the Koranic invocation "Make war... upon such of those to whom the Book has been given until they pay tribute OFFERED on the back of their hands, in a state of humiliation" (9:29). The prominent Arab historian Philip Hitti suggested that campaigns of the early Muslim "seem to have started as raids to provide new outlets for the warring spirit of the tribes now forbidden to engage in fratricidal combats, the objective in most cases being booty and not the gaining of a permanent foothold." Destructive raids pillaged villages, markets, and encampments, gradually weakening neighboring societies, eventually resulting in permanent conquest.

MAPPING ISIS

The developments of June 2014 posed a serious challenge to media cartographers. Some chose simply to depict the individual cities occupied by ISIS. Others connected the dots by stringing together the cities with the roads between them. Still others filled in the blanks with contiguous territory [much of which was sparsely inhabited and had been bypassed by ISIS combatants].

ISIL - BACKGROUND

The Islamic State of Iraq and the Levant (formerly known as Al Qaeda in Iraq - AQI) is one of two al Qaeda affiliates fighting in Syria. AQI is led by Abu Bakr al-Baghdadi, whom the United States has named a Specially Designated Global terrorist. Al-Baghdadi, who is also known as Abu D'ua, is now based in Syria, and has taken personal credit for a series of terrorist attacks in Iraq since 2011.

The Islamic State of Iraq and the Levant [Islamic State of Iraq and al-Sham, al-Sham being an Arab term for the Levant] is by no means the largest of the loosely aligned rebel organizations battling to overthrow Syrian President Bashar al-Assad, and it is concentrated mostly in the northern and eastern provinces of the country. But with its radical ideology and tactics such as kidnappings and beheadings, the group has stamped its identity on the communities in which it is present, including, crucially, areas surrounding the main border crossings with Turkey.

In Iraq, membership was initially estimated between 1,000 and 2,000, making it the largest Sunni violent extremist group in Iraq. Membership in Syria is unknown, although it is likely that the group's members make up a significant portion of the estimated 25,000 violent extremist fighters in Syria. AQI'soperations are predominately Iraq- and Syria-based, but it has perpetrated attacks in Jordan. In Syria, al-Nusrah Front has claimed attacks in several major city centers. AQI maintains a logistical network throughout the Middle East, North Africa, Iran, South Asia, and Europe. AQI receives most of its FUNDING from a variety of businesses and criminal activities within Iraq and Syria.

In 2012, AQI was behind an attack in March on Shia pilgrims in the city of Karbala; the torching of cars near a police headquarters in Kirkuk; the targeting of security forces and government officials in Baghdad; a series of attacks in July that killed 325 people; and attacks in November that killed at least 166 Iraqi civilians, police, and soldiers.

AQI was responsible for the majority of the over 7,000 Iraqi civilians killed in 2013 – the highest number since 2008. In April 2013, AQI's leader Abu Bakr al-Baghdadi declared the group was operating in Syria and changed its public name to the Islamic State of Iraq and the Levant(ISIL). In 2013, ISIL was heavily involved in the fighting in Syria, including against other militant opposition groups, and participated in a number of kidnapping incidents against civilians and reporters. For example, in September ISIL abducted Spanish journalist and photographer, and in December, ISIL reportedly kidnapped at least 120 Kurdish cilvilans in Aleppo province. According to a December 2013 UN report, ISIL is also running secret prisons in northern Syria, where civilians are tortured and killed for challenging ISIL's rule.

In 2013 AQI was responsible for the simultaneous attacks in July 2013 on prisons at al-Taji and Abu Ghraib that killed approximately 29 and freed hundreds of prisoners; a wave of bombings in Baghdad in August that killed approximately 52; and the September bombing of the Kurdistan Democratic Party's Directorate of Security headquarters in Irbil that killed six. On October 6, in Ninewa Province, two Vehicle Borne Improvised Explosive Devices (VBIEDs) were detonated in the al-Aiyathiya neighborhood. The first VBIED was detonated near an elementary school and the second one targeted an Iraqi Police checkpoint. The attacks killed up to 13 school children and one Iraqipolice officer. Another 140 were wounded, mostly students from the school. On October 17, near the end of the Eid al-Adha holiday, a suicide bomber detonated a VBIED in a Shabak minority neighborhood in eastern Mosul, killing 15, including seven children, and woundingmore than 50 others.

On December 23, five people were killed in a suicide bombing after armed AQI militants stormed a television complex in the city of Tikrit. The violence unfolded when a car bomb exploded outside Salah ad Din TV and the local offices of al-Iraqiyya State TV. Militants then stormed the offices of Salah ad Din TV and a suicide bomber killed the chief news editor, a copy editor, a producer, a presenter, and the archives manager. Five other employees were wounded. In April 2013, Al Nusra backers split into two factions:

one group maintained its original name while Abu Bakr al Baghdadi, the leader of AQI, transformed the other faction into a new group called the Islamic State of Iraq and Sham (ISIS). Al Qaedacentral leader Ayman al Zawahiri instructed the groups to refrain from rivalry.

On 09 June 2013 Al-Qaeda's top leader ruled against the merger of two jihadi groups based in Syria and Iraq, in an attempt to put an end to increased tensions and infighting among members. Ayman al-Zawahiri's ruling came in a letter addressed to the leaders of Syrian-based Jabhat al-Nusra and the Islamic State in Iraq (ISI), which is the largest jihadi umbrella group in the country. Al Jazeera exclusively obtained a copy of the letter from reliable sources in Syria. The ruling came two months after the leader of ISI, Abu Bakr al-Baghdadi, declared a merger with al-Nusra to form the Islamic State of Iraq and the Levant (ISIL), saying that al-Nusra was "merely an extension and part of the Islamic State of Iraq". However, the unilateral move led to defections, infighting and a breakdown in operations as members disagreed over who commanded the battlefield.

By September 24, 2013 there was a major firefight along the border, Turkey and Syria, between al-Qaida extremists and forces loyal to Salim Idris. It stretched from Deir Ez Zor down on the southeast part of the country, near the Iraq border, all the way up to the Turkish border north of Aleppo. It was the hardest fighting ever seen between Salim Idris's elements of the Free Syrian Army and the Islamic State of Iraq and the Levant.

The Islamic State of Iraq and the Levant claimed that it overran an air defense base and ammunition depot in Hama province. The ISIL said that "hundreds of the men of the Islamic State" attacked the "Air Defense Battalion and the vital depots of 66th Brigade, and tens of checkpoints, villages, and security points that are spread in the eastern countryside of Hama. The group made the claim in an official statement released yesterday on its official Twitter account; the statement was obtained and translated by the SITE Intelligence Group. The ISIL said that "the soldiers of Allah were able to surprise the enemy from several points in a fashion that it could not imagine, which led to the rapid breakdown of its advanced defenses and the fall of the Air Defense Battalion into the hands of the mujahideen." It claimed that the 66th Brigade's Air Defense Battalion and ammunition depot were overrun after just hours of fighting.

An umbrella group that includes al-Qaida in Iraq, the Islamic State of Iraq and the Levant, (or ISIL), has claimed responsibility for a series of bombings that took place during Eid, when Iraqi families were celebrating the end of the Muslim holy month of Ramadan. Al-Qaeda front group the Islamic State of Iraq and the Levant claimed a wave of attacks that killed 91 people and injured hundreds during the Eid al-Fitr holiday on 11 August 2013. "The Islamic State mobilised... in Baghdad and the southern states and others to convey a quick message of deterrence on the third day of Eid al-Fitr" in response to security forces' operations, a statement posted online said.

IRAQI INSURGENCY GROUPS

The insurgency in Iraq has grown in size and complexity over the course of 2004. Attacks numbered approximately 25 per day at the beginning of 2004, and averaged in the 60s by the end of the year. Insurgents demonstrated their ability to increase attacks around key events such as the Iraqi Interim Government (IIG) transfer of power, Ramadan and the January 2005 election. Attacks on Iraq's election day reached approximately 300, double the previous one day high of approximately 150 reached during Ramadan 2004.

The pattern of attacks remains the same as in 2004. Approximately 80% of all attacks occur.in Sunni-dominated central Iraq. The Kurdish north and Shia south remain relatively calm. Coalition Forces continue to be the primary targets. Iraqi Security Forces and Iraqi Interim Government (IIG) officials are attacked to intimidate the Iraqi people and undermine control and legitimacy. Attacks against foreign nationals are intended to intimidate non-government organizations and contractors and inhibit reconstruction and economic recovery. Attacks against the country's infrastructure, especially electricity and the oil industry, are intended to stall economic recovery, increase popular discontent and further undermine support for the IIG and Coalition. The exact elements attacking the US-led coalition's nation-building effort remain unclear. Since the declared end to major combat operations on 1 May 2003, the continuing attacks against Coalition troops, civilian contractors, aid workers, new Iraqi security forces, as well as the infrastructure, have undermined efforts to reconstruct and stablize the country, carried the total American troop fatality level over 1,000, and led many in the U.S. and elsewhere to question whether the country can be pacified at all without a longer commitment than most consider palatable. Attention has been paid to Saddam loyalists, Iraqi nationalists, foreign Jihadists, militant Sunni and Shia Muslims, and ordinary criminals, with officials trying to assess the nature, goals, funding, and capabilities of the insurgents, the degree of cooperation or conflict between the groups, and links between the insurgency and international terrorist networks and foreign governments.

On 14 November 2003 General John Abizaid, the head of US Central Command, estimated the number of fighters operating against US and allied forces at no more than 5,000, and said the insurgency remained a loosely organized operation. Abizaid said there "is some level of cooperation that's taking place at very high levels, although I'm not sure I'd say there's a national-level resistance leadership." He also said "the most dangerous enemy to us at the present time are the former regime loyalists" operating in central Iraq. According to Abizaid, "The goal of the enemy... is not to defeat us militarily, because they don't have the wherewithal to defeat us militarily. The goal of the enemy is to break the will of the United States of America. It's clear, it's simple, it's straightforward. Break our will, make us leave before Iraq is ready to come out and be a member of the responsible community of nations."

Almost a year on, with kidnappings and beheadings by Islamic militants, large cities still not under the control of coalition forces months away from planned elections, and with security problems requiring the diversion of funds from reconstruction projects, assumptions were being reconsidered and estimates revised. The New York Times reported on 22 October 2004 that senior American officials believed that "hard-core resistance" comprised between 8,000 and 12,000 people, with the number jumping above 20,000 when "active sympathizers or covert accomplices are included." Moreover, officials believed around 50 militant cells were drawing on "unlimited money" through underground networks supplied by people connected with the former regime, as well as wealthy Saudis and Islamic charities. Though some groups had the ability to carry out attacks in regions other than their own, and there may be some degree of cooperation between regions, it is believed that insurgent activities are organized regionally and that no national insurgent network exists.

In January 2005 Iraqi intelligence service director General Mohamed Abdullah Shahwani said that Iraq's insurgency consited of at least 40,000 hardcore fighters, out of a total of more than 200,000 part-time fighters and volunteers who provide intelligence, logistics and shelter. Shahwani said the resistance enjoyed wide backing in the Sunni provinces of Baghdad, Babel, Salahuddin, Diyala, Nineveh and Tamim. Shahwani said the Baath, with a core fighting strength of more than 20,000, had split into three factions. The main one, still owing allegiance to jailed dictator Saddam Hussein, is operating out of Syria. It is led by Saddam's half-brother Sabawi Ibrahim al-Hassan and former aide Mohamed Yunis al-Ahmed, who provide funding to their connections in Mosul, Samarra, Baquba, Kirkuk and Tikrit. Izzat Ibrahim al-Duri is still in Iraq. Two other factions have broken from Saddam, but have yet to mount any attacks. Islamist factions range from Abu Musab al-Zarqawi's al-Qaeda affiliate to Ansar al-Sunna and Ansar al-Islam.

A picture of the composition of the insurgency, though in constant flux, has come into somewhat greater focus. London-based International Institute for Strategic Studies estimates roughly 1,000 foreign Islamic jihadists have joined the insurgency. And there is no doubt many of these have had a dramatic effect on perceptions of the insurgency through high-profile video-taped kidnappings and beheadings. However, American officials believe that the greatest obstacles to stability are the native insurgents that predominate in the Sunni triangle. Significantly, many secular

Sunni leaders were being surpassed in influence by Sunni militant This development mirrors the rise of militant Shia cleric an militia leader Moqtada al-Sadr vis-à-vis the more moderate Shi cleric Grand Ayatollah al-Sistani.

Still, the New York Times article also references military dat suggesting roughly 80 percent of violent attacks in Iraq we simply criminal in nature -e.g., ransom kidnappings and hijackin convoys- and without political motivation. This figure lenc credence to those who cited the CPA's disbanding of the Ira army as an error likely to create a pool of unemployed an discontented young males ripe for absorption into the insurgenc Further, this statistic highlights the importance of reconstructio and the revitalization of an economy in Iraq that can provic traditional employment opportunities. Of the remaining 20 perce of violent attacks -those with political motivation- four-fifths a believed attributable to native insurgents as opposed to foreigne

In late July 2005, Gen. Jack Keane, a former deputy chief staff for the Army, said that US and Iraqi forces had killed captured over 50,000 Iraqi insurgents since the begining of 200 The Pentagon had been previously stated that 15,000 to 16,0 Iraqis were in custody in Iraq. The difference is explained by t fact that some Iraqis who were detained in military operatio were subsequently released.

Former Regime Loyalists [FRL]

Sunni Arabs, dominated by Ba'athist and Former Regin Elements (FRE), comprise the core of the insurgency. Ba'athist/FR and Sunni Arab networks are likely collaborating, providing func and guidance across family, tribal, religious and peer group line

The Former Regime Loyalists, or FRL's, threaten the safety Iraqis and prolong the Coalition presence. By capturing the FRL US Forces are helping Iraq move forward to a peaceful ar prosperous future. Ba'athist loyalists are thought to be responsib for some of the recent attacks against U.S. forces. According to 2 July 2003 Newsweek, two months before the war began, th Mukhabarat, the Iraqi secret police, issued instructions, "to d what's necessary after the fall of the Iraqi leadership to th

American-British-Zionist Coalition forces, God forbid..." The document outlined a total of 11 steps which were to be taken if the U.S. overthrew Saddam's regime. These included "1. Looting and burning government institutions..." In addition, it included orders to sabotaging power plants, and creating chaos by utilizing stolen weapons. The Pentagon has not officially verified this document, according to Newsweek, but has called it "plausible." The current sabatoge and attacks seem to substantiate the possibility that Ba'athist loyalists are responsible for some of the mayhem.

In addition, L. Paul Bremer may have unleashed these former soldiers against US Troops by disbanding the Iraqi military. These former Guard members are without any income, but still are armed and ready to kill, making US Troops vulnerable to attack. While the Republican Guard experienced high casualties in the US strikes on Baghdad, the Special Republican Guard was not especially involved in this part of the war, allowing them to disappear with a number of weapons and munitions. Approximately 40,000 men were members of the Republican Guard. According to the 12 August 2003 New York Times, there is an estimated 100,000 former Iraqi security service members without employment, mostly concentrated in the Sunni Triangle, the same region where many of the attacks have occurred.

Islamic Revivalist

Muslims have been oppressed for decades under the rule of Saddam. While extremist elements are inexperienced in planning attacks, other regional groups are sure to come to their assistance. Such groups include the Al- Faruq Brigades, a militant wing of the Islamic Movement in Iraq (Al-Harakah al-Islamiyyah fi al-arak), the Mujahideen of the Victorious Sect (Mujahideen al ta'ifa al-Mansoura), the Mujahideen Battalions of the Salafi Group of Iraq (Kata'ib al mujahideen fi al-jama'ah al-salafiyah fi al-'arak); and the Jihad Brigades/Cell.

Another insurgency group called "White Flags, Muslim Youth and Army of Mohammed" have claimed responsibility for the attacks against U.S. Forces. The White Flags have urged other Iraqis to attack Americans. In a 10 August 2003 videotape aired on the satellite network Al Arabiya, a Dubai-based station, the White Flags announced that the only way to free Iraq from American occupiers was through guerilla war. "We want to warn countries of the world for the last time not to send troops into Iraq."

Ansar al Islam, a Taliban-like, jihadist group with tie to Al Qaeda is also suspected in guerilla attacks. Before Operation Iraqi Freedom, it was estimated to have 850 members, but nearly 200 were killed by Kurdish and U.S. Special Forces in March. An estimated 300 to 350 fled to Iran during Iraqi freedom, after a few hundred surrendered or were captured.

The 07 May 2003 bombing of the Jordanian Embassy in Iraq has added to speculation that Islamic revivalists, like Ansar al Islam, may be playing a stronger role in the Iraqi insurgency than originally estimated. L. Paul Bremer, the civilian administrator for Iraq, has publically speculated that Ansar al Islam may have been responsible for the car bombing. The attack killed 19 people and wounded more than 60.

One group of Ansar al-Islam militants captured in the Kurdish region during early August 2003 consisted of five Iraqis, a Palestinian and a Tunisian. It was reported that the men had five forged Italian passports for another group of militants. It is estimated that at least 150 members of Ansar al-Islam have entered Iraq with the help of smugglers within the last few weeks. Of the tens of thousands of unemployed former Iraqi security service members, an estimated 2,000 of them, most especially those without any source of income at all, are likely to be recruited by Islamic fundamentalist groups, like Ansar al-Islam.

Recruitment

Recruiting militants has been observed to take place in three stages. First, there is some form of contact initiated, perhaps in a mosque after daily prayers. In this first conversation, a later meeting is arranged. After this meeting, some of the prospective militants are eliminated, leaving the third round of candidates that will train in the campus. Accoring to the 12 August 2003 New York Times, these recruits are instructed to move away from their families and terminate communication with all outsiders.

Foreign fighters are a small component of the insurgency and comprise a very small percentage of all detainees. Syrian, Saudi, Egyptian, Jordanian and Iranian nationals make up the majority of foreign fighters. Fighters, arms and other supplies continue to enter Iraq from virtually all of its neighbors despite increased border security.

Syrian and Iranian Involvement

In December 2004 US General George Casey warned that sympathizers of the insurgency within Syria had been allowed to provide funding, weapons and information to Iraqi insurgents and continued to be a source of infiltration by foreign volunteers.The following February, Iraqi television broadcast taped confessions of alleged insurgents, who claimed to have been trained in Syria, possibly by Syrian intelligence officials. Yet while coalition forces often suspect Syria of assisting insurgents, Syrian denials are adamant and hard evidence is lacking.

Also in February, after continued American pressure, Syria delivered Sabawi Ibrahim Hassan, a half-brother of Saddam and a financial backer of the insurgency. US officials reported some improvement in co-operation against the insurgency from Syria, whose border forces are too few to police the porous Iraqi border effectively. While coalition-aided Iraqi border controls are strengthening, Iraq's bordes, totalling 3,650 kilometres in length, remain difficult to control.

As with Syria, the Iranian presence in Iraq is difficult to guage, although it certainly exists. Several Shi'ite political parties (including SCIRI and al-Da'wa, both members of the United Iraqi Alliance, the country's dominant political coalition), have ties to Iran. The Interim Iraqi Government repeatedly expressed concern over Iraqi influence, Defence Minister Hazem Sha'alan claiming in mid-2004 that there was "clear interference in Iraqi issues by Iran" and that the latter supported terrorism in Iraq. The recalcitrant cleric Muqtada al-Sadr is widely perceived as an Iranian proxy, while in a television interview, Muayed al-Nasseri, commander of Saddam's "Army of Muhhammad," said his group received weapons and cash form both Iran and Syria.

Iran too has strenuously denied involvement. But Iranian actions often diverge from Tehran's official policy: The Iranian polity is fractured, with various power bases supporting their own interests. This was clearly apparent in the aftermath of the capture by Iran in June 2004 of a British patrol boat. After a number of contradictory statements, likely reflecting disagreement between Iranian elements, the crew were released. At the same time, sources within the hard-line Iranian revolutionary made plain that restraint in Iraq was contingent on international treatment of Iran in other aspects of policy, such as Iranian nuclear ambitions, internationally isolated, Iran maintains links with dissidence groups, such as the Lebanese Hizballah, as useful levers in foreign policy negotiation.

IZZAT IBRAHIM AL-DOURI / IZZAT IBRAHIM AL-DURI

Izzat Ibrahim al-Douri was Saddam's number two, Revolution Command Council vice-chairman in the former Iraqi regime, and is now the funder of Sunni insurgents in Iraq. On 13 July 2014 an audio recording emerged that was purportedly from tal-Douri, calling on Iraqis to join efforts to "liberate" the country and praised the offensive by Sunni militants. The voice recording released on a website loyal to Saddam's ousted Baath Party was said to have been made by Ezzat Ibrahim al-Douri, the most senior member of his entourage still at large following Saddam's 2003 overthrow by a U.S.-led invasion force. Although elderly and reported to have been in poor health, Douri is believed to lead the Baathist militant group the Naqshbandi Army, one of several groups which supported the al-Qiada offshoot the Islamic State. "Join the ranks of the rebels who liberated half the country," said the voice on the recording, which resembled previous tapes released in Douri's name. "The liberation of Baghdad is around the corner. Everyone should contribute, to the extent of his ability, to complete the liberation of the beloved country, because there is no honour or dignity without its liberation."

Arriving in Syria in Spring 2003, al-Duri was the highest-ranking Iraqi official in exile. He touted himself as the de facto leader of the Baath Party after Saddam's arrest in 2004, and his main focus was to support the insurgency with funding, people, and material. Al-Duri's ties with Syrian officials reportedly predated the war. Al-Duri was rumored to be a middle man in illicit trade between Saddam's sons Uday and Qusay and former Syrian President Hafez al-Asad's oldest son Basil, who died in a car crash in 1996, and Maher Asad, younger brother to Bashar. Al-Duri is believed to have pocketed a sizable commission from these oil and other deals. Local sources reported in 2004 that al-Duri arrived in Syria with millions of dollars in cash and used that money to buy Syrian influence to establish a base of operations.

Izzat [Ezzet] Ibrahim al-Douri, former vice president of Saddam's revolutionary council, was believed to be behind some attacks against coalition forces and Iraqis. He is the "King of Clubs" No. 6 on the coalition's most-wanted list. Following the capture of Saddam Hussein he became the most wanted man in Iraq. On 23 June 2004 Deputy Secretary Paul Wolfowitz in an interview on MSNBC Hardball said "... it's not insurgency. An insurgency implies something that rose up afterwards. This is the same enemy that butchered Iraqis for 35 years, that fought us up until the fall of Baghdad and continues to fight afterwards. It was led by Saddam Hussein up until his capture in December. It's been led, in part, by his No. 2 or 3, Izzat Ibrahim al Douri, since then."

Jaysh Muhammad (JM) is an anti-Coalition group with both politically motivated and religiously motivated elements. The politically motivated members are Ba'athist, pro-Saddam elements who tend to be of the Sufi religious soca. The Sufi enjoyed special status during the Baath Regime and hold Izzat al-Duri, the ex-vice-president, in exceptionally high esteem. They were members of intelligence, security, and police forces from the previous regime.

The red-haired Ibrahim was born in 1942 near Tikrit. Coming from the same clan area as Saddam, he had no independent power base, and posed no threat to Saddam. Saddam and Ibrahim were among the leading plotters of the 1968 coup which returned the Baath party to power. His daughter was briefly married to Uday Hussein al-Tikriti, a son of President Saddam Hussein.

He was Vice-Chairman of the Revolutionary Command Council (RCC) and Northern Region Commander. He also served as Deputy Secretary General of the Ba'th Party Regional Command and Deputy

Commander of the Armed Forces. After the 1991 Gulf War, he was frequently sent abroad to represent Iraqi interests.

He had a well-deserved and well-known reputation as a killer. As Vice-Chairman of the Revolutionary Command Council, he was complicit in launching two wars of aggression against Iran and Kuwait, invading Saudi Arabia and attacking the town of Khafji in January 1991. He was involved in the brutal repression of the Uprising which followed the Gulf War in 1991 including mass executions, torture and wanton destruction. He was complicit in the deliberate destruction of the Marsh Arabs' way of life. He was also complicit in the genocidal Anfal campaigns waged against the Kurds, including chemical weapons attacks, the destruction of rural villages and infrastructure, and mass executions.

In 1993 the regime embarked on the Return to Faith Campaign (*al-Hamlah al-Imaniyyah*), under the direction of Izzat Ibrahim al-Douri. The Ministry of Endowments and Religious Affairs monitored places of worship, appointed the clergy, approved the building and repair of all places of worship, and approved the publication of all religious literature. The *Imam* (Faith) Campaign allowed Sunni mosques more freedom in practicing religious ceremonies and rites, which reduced substantially the opposition to the regime amongst Sunni Islamists. Forces from the Intelligence Service (Mukhabarat), General Security (Amn al-Amm), the Military Bureau, Saddam's Commandos (Fedayeen Saddam), and the Ba'ath Party killed senior Shi'a clerics, desecrated Shi'a mosques and holy sites (particularly in the aftermath of the 1991 civil uprising), arrested tens of thousands of Shi'a, interfered with Shi'a religious education, prevented Shi'a adherents from performing their religious rites, and fired upon or arrested Shi'a who sought to take part in their religious processions. Security agents were reportedly stationed at all the major Shi'a mosques and shrines and searched, harassed, and arbitrarily arrested worshipers.

On 22 November 1998 Izzat Ibrahim al-Duri escaped an assassination attempt when visiting Karbala. Izzat Ibrahim al-Douri is believed to have been very ill for some years. There are contradictions about his health, and there are some reports that he's trying to put out false information purposely. It is said that he suffers from leukemia and undergoes blood transfusions every six months for treatment. In 1999 he visited Vienna Austria for treatment of leukemia. The Austrian opposition demanded that he be arrested for war crimes, but the government allowed him to leave the country.

In March 2003 he commanded military forces in the north of Iraq during the U.S. invasion last year. On 05 September 2003 it was reported that Izzat Ibrahim al-Douri had been captured in the town of Tikrit. However, within hours, the US-led coalition denied they had him in custody. The error was particularly embarrassing because Iraqi officials had chosen to break the news to *al-Hurra,* the new US-funded satellite channel which was intended to bring reliable and credible news to the Arab world.

Anonymous US Government officials claimed in October 2003 that captured members of Ansar al-Islam had said that Izzat Ibrahim al-Douri was helping to coordinate their attacks on US occupation forces. In November 2003 the Coalition launched a public information campaign across Iraq to promote a $10 million reward for information that will lead to his capture or killing al-Douri. On 29 November 2003 the wife and daughter of Izzat Ibrahim al-Douri were arrested in Samarra. The US military detained some of his family members and the son of his doctor in an attempt to pressure him to surrender.

On 16 December 2003 there was a report on Al-Arabiyya Television based in Dubai that Izzat Ibrahim al-Douri, may have surrendered. This reported turned out to be incorrect. In the northeast zone of operations, a cordon-and-search operation on 04 January 2004 in Mosul led to the capture of an associate of Izzat Ibrahim al-Douri and 11 other personnel. Upon leaving the area, the unit was attacked by six personnel, but the coalition unit, while returning fire, broke contact in order to safeguard the lives of the detainees. Iraq's Coalition Provisional Authority Administrator Paul Bremer said 07 January 2004 that a reward of $10 million will be given for information leading to the capture of — or confirmation regarding the death of — Izzat Ibrahim al-Douri. Searching two locations near Hawija during the morning of 13 January 2004, 173rd Airborne Brigade soldiers captured 10 people for conducting anti-Coalition activities. Four of the individuals, captured in cordon-and-knock operations in Mosul, 2 kilometers north of Hawija, were targeted in order to prevent them from interfering with future Coalition operations. A person believed to be a money courier for Izzat Ibrahim Al Duri and three others were captured in a raid conducted by 173rd Airborne Brigade soldiers in Kirkuk in the early morning of 13 January 2004. The four brothers [al-Douri's nephews] were captured without incident.

On 07 March 2004, members of 4th Platoon, Charlie Troop, 1-4 CAV conducted Charlie Troop's first raid to detain three personnel with connections to High Value Target #6 Izzat Ibrahim Al Duri. All three were detained at their three different locations without incident and turned them over for interrogation.

On 05 September 2004 a man who resembled Izzat Ibrahim Al Duri was arrested in Tikrit. Iraqi Minister of State Wael Abdul al-Latif said it was "75 to 90 per cent certain" the captured man was al-Douri. Some 70 of the man's supporters were killed and 80 captured when they tried to prevent his arrest. Iraqi officials said the arrest operation began when Mr. al-Douri was receiving medical treatment at a clinic in Tikrit, and that he may suffer from leukemia. Celebratory gunfire erupted in the streets of the Iraqi capital Baghdad as word of his arrest was spread. Blood tests were conducted to confirm his identity. The DNA tests performed to determine the identity of the captive indicated that not actually al-Douri. Iraq's Defense minister dismissed as "baseless" reports that Iraqi forces have captured one of the most wanted members of Saddam Hussein's ousted dictatorship. In an interview Hazem Shaalan said the defense ministry has "no information" regarding the alleged arrest of Izzat Ibrahim al-Douri.

Al-Duri's whereabouts between 2003 and 2009 remain difficult to pin down, but many observers in Syria believe he traveled in and out of Syria frequently. Al-Duri claimed in July 2006 that the Baath Party was responsible for "95 percent" of the insurgency in Iraq and criticized al-Qaeda/Iraq Abu Musab al-Zarqawi for seeking to instill "hateful sectarianism." Despite this anti-Islamic bias, Al-Duri's focus on supporting the insurgency may have led him to establish links to al-Qaeda networks using Syria to pass jihadis into Iraq, but most of the evidence for such links remains anecdotal. Al-Duri traveled around the region and in Iraq itself. *A Nov. 11, 2005 statement attributed to Iraq's ousted Baath Party reported that Izzat Ibrahim al-Douri had died that day, possibly from Leukemia from which he had been known to suffer from since the late 1990s. The reports of his death were greatly exagerated.* He was reportedly killed in Iraq in November 2005 but then later emerged quite alive in a press interview. Al-Duri then resurfaced in Syria in 2008 just as Syrian-Iraqi relations were beginning to improve. In press remarks attributed to him in May 2008, al-Douri criticized Syria for not providing sufficient support to the "Baath cause," prompting a public rebuke from Syrian FM Muallim. Muallim reportedly told Iraqi officials in March 2009 that al-Duri was no longer welcome in Syria. al-Douri spoke in an audiotape broadcast 07 April 2009 on Al-Jazeera television, in which he urged his followers to topple the government of Prime Minister Nouri al-Maliki after the US withdrawal from the country. In March 2009 Baath party hardliners led by Izzat Ibrahim al-Duri, were reported to reject reconciliation and to have vowed to fight the "traitors" to the finish. At that time it was reported that Iraqi intelligence sources emphasized that Izzat al-Duri was hiding in one of the strongholds of the so-called "the Islamic State of Iraq" in the southern suburbs of Diyala, northeast of Baghdad.

JAYSH MUHAMMAD

Jaysh Muhammad (The Army of Muhammad) (JM) is an anti-Coalition group with both politically motivated and religiously motivated elements. By late 2004 it appeared that the politically motivated members are Ba'athist, pro-Saddam elements who tend to be of the Sufi religious soca. The Sufi enjoyed special status during the Regime and hold Izzat al-Duri, the ex-vice-president, in exceptionally high esteem. They were members of intelligence, security, and police forces from the previous regime.

Jaysh Muhammad was initially believed to consist of terrorists who have infiltrated Iraq from Saudi Arabia and other Arab countries. By early 2004 it was believed to have formed an alliance with former intelligence and security agents of Saddam Hussein to fight the US forces. This alliance was is believed to be responsible for increasingly sophisticated attacks on US soldiers in early 2004. It is not clear how these elements may be cooperating, or whether there are separate centers of initiative. While *Jaysh Muhammad* is one of several names seek to imply a religious element that have claimed for car bombings, but the name can be deceiving and may be a false flag.

The Iraqi *Jaysh Muhammad* should not be confused with the Pakistani group called *Jaish-e-Muhammad*. The Pakistani group is led by Akbar Agha, who is known to have been close to Osama bin Laden. By July 2003 attacks on coalition troops were being carried out by numerous Islamist groups. These resistance operations were not linked to Saddam Hussein. The Islamist groups involved included *Ansar Al-Islam* [Supporters of Islam], *Jund Al-Islam* [Soldiers of Islam], *Jaysh Muhammad* [Muhammad's Army], and other extremist groups.

A masked man claiming to speak for the Islamic Jihad Brigades of Muhammad's Army (Jaysh Muhammad), Abdallah Bin-Iyad Brigade, took responsibility for the 19 August bombing of the UN compound in Baghdad in an audiotape provided to Lebanon's LBC satellite television on 23 August 2003. A group calling itself the Armed Vanguards of the Second Muhammad Army claimed responsibility for the bombing of the UN headquarters in Baghdad, The claim took the form of a typewritten, Arabic statement shown on the Al-Arabiya station on 21 August 2003.

On 31 January 2004 men with their faces covered distributed circulated a declaration in al-Fallujah outlining their plan for taking control of Iraqi cities after the US occupation forces withdraw. The declaration was signed by 12 organizations and groups including: The Iraqi Islamic Patriotic Resistance [*al-Muqawamah al-Wataniyah al-Islamiyah al-'Iraqiyah*], the Salafi Movement for Propagation and Jihad [*al-Harakah as-Salafiyah li-d-Da'wah wa-l-Jihad*], the al-Qari'ah Organization [*Tanzim al-Qari'ah*], the Army of Partisans of the Sunnah [*Jaysh Ansar as-Sunnah*], and the Army of Muhammad [*Jaysh Muhammad*].

An anonymous interview with a member of Iraq's *Jaysh Muhammad* from Ba'qubah gave to the Institute of War and Peace

Reporting was published on 14 May 2004. The source stated that the majority of Jaysh Muhammad combatants are farmer workers who joined the Salafist Sunni movement to drive the coalition from Iraq. He said there were only a few foreign fighters in the group and that they had "lived with us [before the war] and did not come from abroad after the war." He denied that the group, which he described as not Wahhabi, is linked to Al-Qaeda. He also claimed that the group received no funding from abroad, but that it is funded "from honorable and good people in this country." He said that *Jaysh Muhammad* opposed the Iraqi Governing Council because it was not elected, and since so many of the Council members were exiles. "They do not understand Iraqis' suffering and Arab traditions. [They] were distorted by the Western life they lived," he said. He also claimed that his group is affiliated with an Islamic political party, but declined to identify which party, only to say that it is not the Iraqi Islamic Party. While he denied the group targeted Iraq police officere, he condoned the kidnapping of foreigners, saying that "kidnapping is an obligation." He also said: "There is no real United Nations. It is an organization completely controlled by the United States and its resolutions always serve U.S. interests."

THE ISIL'S STAND IN THE RAMADI-FALLUJA CORRIDOR

Since December 30, 2013, the Islamic State in Iraq and the Levant (ISIL) has sought to carve out an area of control in the Iraqi cities of Ramadi and Falluja, as well as in the Euphrates River delta between these urban areas. These locations are replete with symbolic and strategic significance for the ISIL. The movement's forerunner, al-Qa'ida in Iraq (AQI), fought in the iconic twin battles for Falluja in March and November 2004, an event that fanned the flames of Iraq's Sunni insurgency for years afterwards. In late 2006, Anbar tribes turned decisively against AQI and its affiliates in the provincial capital of Ramadi, beginning the movement's near-fatal deterioration. These cities and their outlying rural satellites continue to be key terrain: the Ramadi-Falluja corridor is just 22 miles from the capital's international airport and sits astride the country's main trucking highways to Jordan and Syria. Iraqi security forces have been excluded from Falluja—a city with a population of more than 300,000 on Baghdad's doorstep—for nearly five months.

This article recounts how the ISIL spread into Ramadi and Falluja, why it has failed to secure control of Ramadi, and the conditions that have led to its present control of Falluja. It finds that while the ISIL's activities in the Ramadi-Falluja corridor are concerning, the extent of the movement's real control of the area is debatable. Furthermore, the ISIL may have overreached by committing itself to the defense of terrain, particularly in urban areas so close to the Iraqi government's logistical bases around Baghdad. If current trends continue, the ISIL's gambit in the Ramadi-Falluja corridor could bring a strategic reversal for the movement within the Iraqi theater.

Opening Moves

Throughout 2013, the Iraqi government had chafed at the existence of two "Arab Spring"-style Sunni Arab protest sites in Ramadi and Falluja. On December 28, 2013, the influential Iraqi cleric `Abd al-Malik al-Sa`di issued a statement from Jordan calling on Sunnis to defend the protest camp, which government forces were massing against. Armed tribal forces were fully mobilized by December 30, when Iraqi forces suspended local cellphone and internet communications and began to bulldoze the Ramadi and Falluja protest sites. Al-Sa`di called on security force members to defect and for all Sunnis to rise up. Tribal forces in northern Ramadi repelled Iraqi Army 1st division troops from the sit-in square. Tribal fighters also routed newly-arrived Emergency Response Brigade forces from various police stations in Ramadi city. The arrival of these predominately Shi`a forces from the southern city of Kut stoked tensions and contributed to the tribal backlash. To restore calm, the Ramadi-based Anbar provincial council negotiated a withdrawal of Iraqi Army and Emergency Response Brigade forces from Ramadi on December 31. Entering Ramadi from multiple directions on January 1, 2014, ISIL fighters opportunistically exploited the breakdown of government control to ransack police stations in the city.

The dynamic was markedly different in Falluja where (even before the crisis) Iraqi Army forces were normally only located on the outer edges of the city. From the night of December 30, armed locals also came to the streets, massing at the main Falluja protest site (on the highway east of the urban center), appearing to answer earlier calls by 'Abd al-Malik al-Sa'di and Grand Mufti Sheikh Rafi' al-Rifa'i to block the road to prevent reinforcements from reaching Ramadi and western Anbar. Local residents also fortified the entry checkpoints to the city to exclude Iraqi government forces from entering Falluja. After some days of inconclusive skirmishing around the edges of Falluja city, Iraqi government forces settled down for a prolonged siege. Inside the city, ISIL convoys paraded in Falluja's streets, ransacking local police stations and using megaphones to call on residents to repent and pledge allegiance. The ISIL unilaterally declared Falluja an Islamic state at Friday prayers on January 3, 2014.

The ISIL in Ramadi

In Ramadi, the provincial government and key tribal groupings were loosely aligned with the government against the ISIL until the government arrest and military operations of December 28-30, 2013. Almost immediately after the late December clashes, the government and most of Ramadi's tribes once again made common cause against the ISIL, seemingly in reaction to the ISIL's alarming expansion into Ramadi city neighborhoods. The ISIL's northern effort failed in January 2014. The ISIL fighters from the Western Euphrates River Valley towns and the Western Desert reinforced the ISIL in the rural areas north of Ramadi such as Albu Sha'ban and 'Ali Jassim, and to the 'Alwan and Albu Fahad tribal areas to the northeast of Ramadi. By the end of January, locally-recruited police paramilitaries, tribal fighters and the military pacified the urban areas of Ramadi north of the Euphrates collectively known as Albu Faraj or Jazira.

The situation in southern Ramadi evolved very differently, with the ISIL mounting a costly multi-month effort to dominate the southern neighborhoods of al-Mal'ab, Fursan, Hayy al-Dhubat and al-Hawz. This effort was launched from al-Humayra and Albu Jabr, a belt of rural suburbs south of the train line that marks Ramadi city's southern edge. The area is physically linked to similar ISIL "support zones" south of Falluja and stretching down to the Jurf as-Sakhar area in northern Babil Province. The ISIL has been strident in its defense of its southern launch-pads.

In al-Humayra, for example, an Iraqi Army probe was decimated on April 20, 2014, by wire-guided anti-tank missiles, with the loss of an entire mixed platoon of T-62 tanks and MTLB armored vehicles. ISIL forces have used titanium-coated, armor-piercing ammunition in Dragonov-model rifles to shoot out the engine blocks on large numbers of Iraqi Hummers in an apparent effort to reduce Iraqi Security Force (ISF) mobility. When security forces began searches for ISIL workshops in late March 2014, a car bomb damaged the bridge linking Ramadi city to the al-Ta'mim suburb, the historic site for ISIL bombmaking workshops in Ramadi.

The determination of the ISIL's efforts to destabilize southern Ramadi are quite exceptional, even by the violent standards of today's Iraq.

Prior to the late summer of 2013, the ISIL conducted around eight to ten attacks per month in Ramadi's urban center south of the Euphrates. This increased to an average of 20 attacks per month from September-December 2013, reflecting an intensification of attacks on police forces and tribal leaders. From January-April 2014, the average number of monthly attacks surged to 44 in the southern Ramadi neighborhoods.

The destructiveness of the attacks also increased, causing significant material damage and major outflows of internally displaced persons. In 2013, there was an average of one attempted mass casualty attack in Ramadi per month: in the first four months of 2014, the monthly average increased to 9.25. In April 2014, the ISIL launched 13 attempted suicide vest attacks and six attempted suicide car bombings in southern Ramadi.

The ISIL has INVESTED significant numbers of suicide militants to keep the fight active in Ramadi, despite the low probability that the ISIL will eventually control the city. Ramadi city was the heart of the tribal "awakening" in Iraq and the ISIL appears determined to keep fighting in this area. It has succeeded, in so far as ongoing violence is a distraction to the government and prolongs the sense that the city is contested. Yet Ramadi is essentially under government control, albeit with a significant "commuter insurgency" still able to penetrate the city's southern flank and repeatedly draw the government into destructive clearance operations.

This is arguably a limited payoff for a significant investment of ISIL effort and presumably considerable losses as well. If the ISIL downgrades its effort or loses its southern Ramadi support zone, the government and its tribal allies may be able to claim a partial victory.

The ISIL's Stand in Falluja

The background to the ISIL's creeping takeover of Falluja is rooted in the city's isolated status within Anbar Province. Falluja is an insular town renowned for its rebelliousness and links to Salafism.

The tribal uprising that gathered momentum in Ramadi never achieved the same result in Falluja, and al-Qa'ida affiliates have enjoyed far greater ongoing freedom of movement in Falluja, including at the city's protest camps. Throughout 2013, the ISIL sought to expand its profile inside Falluja city.

Militant attacks claimed by the ISIL in Falluja city rose from an average of 16 per month in the first quarter of 2013 to 31 in the last quarter of that year, with an apex of 39 incidents in December 2013. The ISIL's preferred tactics in Falluja throughout the year were drive-by shootings, under-vehicle bombings and car bombings of houses belonging to local leaders and police forces. The ISIL also targeted electrical generator operators, shopkeepers and clerics in a slow-building campaign of fundraising and influence-building.

Throughout 2013, the ISIL also strengthened its hold on the southern neighborhoods and southern rural outskirts of Falluja city. The Euphrates River communities south of Falluja such as al-N'imiya and 'Amiriy were important AQI support zones in 2006 until the local Albu 'Issa tribes sought U.S. support to break al-Qa'ida's stranglehold. Since then, the ISIL has gradually clawed its way back into these areas. An ISIL suicide bomber killed the key anti-ISIL tribal leader, Shaykh 'Aifan al-'Issawi, in January

2013. The consolidation in 2013 of the ISIL's "Wilayat al-Janub" in the Jurf as-Sakhar area of northern Babil has placed another contiguous support zone to the southeast. By October 19, 2013, the ISIL was confident enough to hold a 50 vehicle rally in daylight in the southern Falluja mechanics area of al-Shuhada', a historical car bomb manufacturing hub. An ISIL sniper killed Falluja's mayor, 'Adnan Hussein al-Dulaymi, in al-Shuhada' on November 13, 2013.

One of the most interesting aspects of the Falluja stand-off in 2014 has been the state of relations between the ISIL and other insurgent factions within the city. On the surface, the groups have cooperated, with non-ISIL forces manning many of the city's perimeter defenses and with the ISIL providing military support and advice.

The relationship, however, is more complex: Fallujans never rejected al-Qa'ida and its spin-offs to the extent that Ramadi's tribes did. Even so, memories of the destruction that al-Qa'ida brought upon the city in 2004 are still fresh.

There is also considerable bitterness between former AQI fighters and Fallujans who cooperated with the government, notably tribal groups like the Albu 'Issa and the Iraqi Islamic Party (IIP) with its militant wing in Falluja, Hamas al-Iraq. Initially, the ISIL struck a conciliatory note, promising not to attack the locally-recruited police forces and merely chiding Fallujans for backing the government against AQI from 2007 onwards.

Very quickly, however, the ISIL escalated its contest with the IIP and Hamas al-Iraq. In early January 2014, most of the Falluja police force ceased wearing uniforms and police stations associated with former Hamas al-Iraq members were abandoned to ISIL looting.

From January 3 onwards, ISIL patrols cruised Falluja city in captured police vehicles using megaphones to call policemen to repent. The ISIL reacted aggressively when the Iraqi government and Ramadi shaykhs negotiated the appointment of a new mayor and police chief for Falluja on January 12: throughout the latter half of January, the ISIL detained and harassed the new mayor, damaged the mayor's office with multiple improvised explosive devices (IEDs), and bombed the new police chief's home.

Although the ISIL agreed not to hold rallies or try to govern the city when it joined the Falluja Military Council on February 8, 2014, the movement has consistently overstepped the reported restrictions placed upon it by other Fallujan rebels. For example, on March 20, the ISIL held a major rally in Falluja's government center that included ISIL flags carried on captured police vehicles and Iraqi Army Hummers.

In the April 24-30 period, the ISIL undertook house demolitions against the Falluja homes of three Anbar provincial council members and one member of parliament. National elections proved impossible to hold in Falluja on April 30. The ISIL has also sought to take over distribution of critical supplies including food and cooking gas bottles. At the start of May, the Falluja Military Council publicly complained that the ISIL was disarming rival militias inside Falluja rather than focusing fully on the defense of the city against the common enemy, the Iraqi government. The tone of the council's complaints indicates that the ISIL is increasingly in charge within Falluja.

The federal government was initially willing to contain the ISIL within Falluja rather than risk a political and military setback during the electoral and government formation processes. This option has been undermined by the porous cordon around Falluja city and by the ISIL's determination to launch strategic high-impact attacks toward Baghdad.

One theme touted by the ISIL has been a renewed battle of Baghdad, a city where the Sunni minority and its militias were roundly defeated and purged in many areas by Shi'a militias in 2006-2007.

On January 19, 2014, ISIL amir Abu Bakr al-Baghdadi urged fighters to "creep toward Baghdad," a call that was later echoed on April 12 in a communiqué to slip "as soft as fog" into Baghdad. With surprising mobility, the ISIL appears to have moved forces from its Ramadi-Falluja corridor and the shores of Lake Tharthar to Baghdad's outskirts via Saqlawiya, Karma and Abu Ghurayb. On March 31, the ISIL held a large parade in an outer suburb of Abu Ghurayb comprising between 70-100 vehicles, including Iraqi Army Hummers and even an M113 tracked armored personnel carrier. On April 9, the U.S. government warned about a threat to Baghdad International Airport, adjacent to Abu Ghurayb.

Using a different approach, the ISIL also manipulated its on-off control of the regulating dams downstream of Falluja to flood the Euphrates delta from April 6 onwards, causing extensive displacement of rural residents and threatening to flood metropolitan Baghdad. These gambits, alongside the well-publicized execution of Iraqi special forces, appear to have been designed to lure the Iraqi military into a hasty assault on Falluja, a potential spark for a wider Sunni Arab uprising against the government. With Iraqi forces tightening the siege and clearing Falluja's rural outskirts on all sides during May 2014, the ISIL may have succeeded in speeding up the government's plans for Falluja.

Conclusion

The ISIL, and its predecessor the ISI, has been remarkably successful in recovering its position in Iraq since 2011, yet the movement's Iraqi successes cannot yet compare to its development of a secure capital city in al-Raqqa, Syria. Iraq is still a FINANCIAL powerhouse for the ISIL, particularly its third-largest city, Mosul, but the ISIL's political center of gravity is undoubtedly in Syria. The ISIL's ambitions in the Ramadi-Falluja corridor represent a potential shift in this dynamic, with the movement seeking to establish long-term control over liberated zones at the heart of Iraq. If successful, the development of a defensible ISIL caliphate just outside Baghdad would be a historic achievement on par with anything the movement has achieved in Syria. Such success would be doubly sweet, taking place on iconic terrain where the ISIL's predecessors experienced great success in 2004 and crushing defeat in 2006-2007.

This intoxicating vision comes with a warning: the ISIL has now committed itself to a battle for terrain, and the fight is taking place at a point where the Iraqi military can easily concentrate and supply its forces and where local allies may be willing to enable the government's offensive. At the present time, there are reportedly 13 Iraqi military brigades with extensive artillery and air support deployed in the Ramadi-Falluja corridor. Baghdad International

Airport provides a secure resupply route for the significant U.S. military aid being provided to Iraq's forces. The ISIL may have placed itself on an anvil. If the hammer falls and the government mismanages its offensive, causing significant civilian casualties or failing to evict the ISIL, the militant group will score an important victory. Yet the ISIL now faces the same strategic puzzle as forerunners such as AQI: it needs to either control territory or it may begin to fade away in the face of local pushback. If the government can pacify Ramadi and Falluja, particularly with local tribes in the lead, then the ISIL could experience a very public strategic setback. For the ISIL project in Iraq, the Ramadi-Falluja conflict could be a fulcrum point.

4

Syria-Iraq: The Islamic State Militant and Terror

Islamic State stands with al-Qaeda as one of the most dangerous jihadist groups, after its gains in Syria and Iraq. Under its former name Islamic State in Iraq and the Levant (ISIS), it was formed in April 2013, growing out of al-Qaeda in Iraq (AQI). It has since been disavowed by al-Qaeda, but has become one of the main jihadist groups fighting government forces in Syria and Iraq.

Its precise size is unclear but it is thought to include thousands of fighters, including many foreign jihadists. The organisation is led by Abu Bakr al-Baghdadi. Little is known about him, but it is believed he was born in Samarra, north of Baghdad, in 1971 and joined the insurgency that erupted in Iraq soon after the 2003 US-led invasion. In 2010 he emerged as the leader of al-Qaeda in Iraq, one of the groups that later became ISIS.

Baghdadi is regarded as a battlefield commander and tactician, which analysts say makes his group more attractive to young jihadists than al-Qaeda, which is led by Ayman al-Zawahiri, an Islamic theologian. Prof Peter Neumann of King's College London estimates that about 80% of Western fighters in Syria have joined the group. IS claims to have fighters from the UK, France, Germany and other European countries, as well as the US, the Arab world and the Caucasus.

Unlike other rebel groups in Syria, IS is seen to be working towards an Islamic emirate that straddles Syria and Iraq. The group has seen considerable military success. In March 2013, it took over the Syrian city of Raqqa - the first provincial capital to fall under rebel control. In January 2014, it capitalised on growing tension between Iraq's Sunni minority and Shia-led government by taking control of the predominantly Sunni city of Fallujah, in the western province of Anbar.

It also seized large sections of the provincial capital, Ramadi, and has a presence in a number of towns near the Turkish and Syrian borders. The group has gained a reputation for brutal rule in the areas that it controls. However, it was its conquest of Mosul in June that sent shockwaves around the world. The US said the fall of Iraq's second city posed a threat to the entire region. It may also have made ISIS the most cash-rich militant group in the world.

Initially, the group relied on donations from wealthy individuals in Gulf Arab states, particularly Kuwait and Saudi Arabia, who supported its fight against President Bashar al-Assad. Today, IS is said to earn significant amounts from the oil fields it controls in eastern Syria, reportedly selling some of the supply back to the Syrian government. It is also believed to have been selling looted antiquities from historical sites. Prof Neumann believes that before the capture of Mosul in June 2014, IS had cash and assets worth about $900m (£500m). Afterwards, this rose to around $2bn (£1.18bn). The group reportedly took hundreds of millions of dollars from Mosul's branch of Iraq's central bank. And its financial windfall looked set to continue if it maintains control of oil fields in northern Iraq.

Inter-rebel Tension

The group has been operating independently of other jihadist groups in Syria such as the al-Nusra Front, the official al-Qaeda affiliate in the country, and has had a tense relationship with other rebels. Baghdadi sought to merge with al-Nusra, which rejected the deal, and the two groups have operated separately since. Zawahiri has urged IS to focus on Iraq and leave Syria to al-Nusra, but Baghdadi and his fighters openly defied the al-Qaeda chief. Hostility to IS grew steadily in Syria as regularly attacked fellow rebels and abused civilian supporters of the Syrian opposition. In

January 2014, rebels from both Western-backed and Islamist groups launched an offensive against IS, seeking to drive its predominantly foreign fighters out of Syria. Thousands of people are reported to have been killed in the infighting.

ISLAMIC STATE IN IRAQ AND THE LEVANT

With its multi-pronged assault across central and northern Iraq in the past one and a half weeks, the Islamic State of Iraq and the Levant (ISIS) has taken over from the al-Qa'ida organisation founded by Osama bin Laden as the most powerful and effective extreme jihadi group in the world. ISIS now controls or can operate with impunity in a great stretch of territory in western Iraq and eastern Syria, making it militarily the most successful jihadi movement ever.

While its exact size is unclear, the group is thought to include thousands of fighters. The last "s" of "ISIS" comes from the Arabic word "al-Sham", meaning Levant, Syria or occasionally Damascus, depending on the circumstances. Led since 2010 by Abu Bakr al-Baghdadi, also known as Abu Dua, it has proved itself even more violent and sectarian than what US officials call the "core" al-Qa'ida, led by Ayman al-Zawahiri, who is based in Pakistan.

ISIS is highly fanatical, killing Shia Muslims and Christians whenever possible, as well as militarily efficient and under tight direction by top leaders. The creation of a sort of proto-Caliphate by extreme jihadis in northern Syria and Iraq is provoking fears in surrounding countries such as Jordan, Saudi Arabia and Turkey that they will become targets of battle-hardened Sunni fighters.

The ISIS tactic is to make a surprise attack, inflict maximum casualties and spread fear before withdrawing without suffering heavy losses. Last Friday they attacked Mosul, where their power is already strong enough to tax local businesses, from family groceries to mobile phone and construction companies. Some 200 people were killed in the fighting, according to local hospitals, though the government gives a figure of 59 dead, 21 of them policemen and 38 insurgents. ISIS specialises in using militarily untrained foreign volunteers as suicide bombers either moving on foot wearing suicide vests, or driving vehicles packed with explosives. Often more than one suicide bomber is used, as happened when a vehicle exploded at the headquarters of a Kurdish party, the Patriotic Union of Kurdistan in the town of Jalawla in the divided and much fought-over province of Diyala, north-east of Baghdad. In the confusion caused by the blast, a second bomber on foot slipped into the office and blew himself up, killing some 18 people, including a senior police officer.

The swift rise of ISIS since Abu Bakr al-Baghdadi became its leader has come because the uprising of the Sunni in Syria in 2011 led the Iraqi Sunni to protest about their political and economic marginalisation since the fall of Saddam Hussein. Peaceful demonstrations from the end of 2012 won few concessions, with Iraq's Shia-dominated government convinced that the protesters wanted not reform but a revolution returning their community to power. The five or six million Iraqi Sunni became more alienated and sympathetic towards armed action by ISIS.

An undated picture released by Iraq's Interior Ministry claiming to show ISIS leader Abu Bakr al-Baghdadi ISIS launched a well-planned campaign last year including a successful assault on Abu Ghraib prison last summer to free leaders and experienced fighters. This January, they took over Fallujah, 40 miles west of Baghdad, and have held it ever since in the face of artillery and air attack. The military sophistication of ISIS in Iraq is much greater than al-Qa'ida, the organisation out of which it grew, which reached the peak of its success in 2006-07 before the Americans turned many of the Sunni tribes against it.

ISIS has the great advantage of being able to operate on both sides of the Syrian-Iraq border, though in Syria it is engaged in an intra-jihadi civil war with Jabhat al-Nusra, Ahrar al-Sham and other groups. But ISIS controls Raqqa, the only provincial capital taken by the opposition, and much of eastern Syria outside enclaves held by the Kurds close to the Turkish border.

ISIS is today a little more circumspect in killing all who work for the government including rubbish collectors, something that alienated the Sunni population previously. But horrifically violent, though professionally made propaganda videos show ISIS forcing families with sons in the Iraqi army to dig their own graves before they are shot. The message is that their enemies can expect no mercy.

Who is ISIS leader Abu Bakr al-Baghdadi?

In the space of a year he has become the most powerful jihadi leader in the world, and last week his forces captured Mosul, the northern capital of Iraq. Abu Bakr al-Baghdadi, also known as Abu Dua, the leader of the Islamic State of Iraq and the Levant (ISIS) has suddenly emerged as a figure who is shaping the future of Iraq, Syria and the wider Middle East.

He began to appear from the shadows in the summer of 2010 when he became leader of al-Qa'ida in Iraq (AQI) after its former leaders were killed in an attack by US and Iraqi troops. AQI was at a low point in its fortunes, as the Sunni rebellion, in which it had once played a leading role, was collapsing. It was revived by the revolt of the Sunni in Syria in 2011 and, over the next three years by a series of carefully planned campaigns in both Iraq and Syria. How far al-Baghdadi is directly responsible for the military strategy and tactics of ISIS, once called AQI, is uncertain: former Iraqi army and intelligence officers from the Saddam era are said to play a crucial role, but are under al-Baghdadi's overall leadership.

There are disputes over his career depending on whether the source is ISIS itself, US or Iraqi intelligence but the overall picture appears fairly clear. He was born in Samarra, a largely Sunni city north of Baghdad, in 1971 and is well educated. With black hair and brown eyes, a picture of al-Baghdadi taken when he was a prisoner of the Americans in Bocca Camp in southern Iraq between 2005 and 2009, makes him look like any Iraqi man in his thirties.

His real name is believed to be Awwad Ibrahim Ali al-Badri al-Samarrai, who has degrees in Islamic Studies, including poetry, history and genealogy, from the Islamic University of Baghdad. He may have been an Islamic militant under Saddam as a preacher in Diyala province, to the north east of Baghdad, where, after the US invasion of 2003, he had his own armed group. Insurgent movements have a strong motive for giving out misleading information about their command structure and leadership, but it appears al-Baghdadi spent five years as prisoner of the Americans.

After the old AQI leadership was killed in April 2010, al-Baghdadi took over and AQI became increasingly well organised, even issuing detailed annual reports over the last two years, itemising its operations in each Iraqi province. Recalling the fate of his predecessors as AQI leader, he insisted on extreme secrecy, so few people knew where he was. AQI prisoners either say they have never met him or, when they did, that he was wearing a mask.

Taking advantage of the Syrian civil war, al-Baghdadi sent experienced fighters and funds to Syria to set up Jabhat al-Nusra as al-Qa'ida's affiliate in Syria. He split from it last year, but remains in control of a great swathe of territory in northern Syria and Iraq. Against fragmented and dysfunctional opposition, he is moving fast towards establishing himself as Emir of a new Islamic state.

HOW ISIL IS FUNDED, TRAINED AND OPERATING IN IRAQ AND SYRIA?

Islamic State and the Levant is a growing terrorist organisation, but just who are they and where does their money come from? Islamic State and the Levant is growing financially and militarily but their greatest financial triumph came in June when they captured Mosul. But how is the group funded and how did their capabilities increase?

Funding & Resources

ISIL is the richest terrorist organisation in history. Over the past six months, since the group began sweeping across eastern Syria and into Iraq, experts estimate that its leaders have gained access to £1.2 billion in cash – more than the most recent recorded annual military expenditure of Ireland. "ISIL is not out in the economic boondocks of Afghanistan or hidden in deserts and caves," said Paul Sullivan, a Middle East specialist at Georgetown University in Washington. "ISIL is developing in a vital oil, gas and trade area of the world. It can grab as it expands." Their greatest financial triumph came when they captured the Iraqi town of Mosul in June and looted the city's banks. Reports at the time suggested the group's fighters may have made off with £240 million, though the Iraqi government later said the heist did not occur.

Five captured oilfields provide up to £1.8 million per day in revenue, with much of the oil smuggled across the border into Turkey and Iran. They are thought to earn up to £5 million a month through extortion of local businesses. In the past year they are estimated to have made £40 million from taking hostages, with each foreign hostage thought to be worth £3m – although the kidnappers of American journalist James Foley demanded £80 million. Private donations from supporters in the Gulf also contribute to their funding – although Saudi Arabia and other Gulf nations have tried to make it harder to do so without government approval. During the war in Afghanistan, Saudi supporters could donate money directly at their mosque with no government supervision.

When they captured Mosul, Iraq's envoy to the UN said they obtained nearly 88lb (40kg) of nuclear material, in the form of low-grade uranium compounds seized from a scientific research facility. The nuclear material would not be easily turned into weapons. After conquering swaths of western Iraq, ISIL fighters also now control territory where 40 per cent of the country's wheat is grown. The group's members are also reportedly milling grain in government silos and selling the flour on the local market.

Tactics & Targets

ISIL's strategy is to capture cities, occupy civilian homes, and expand their vision of a Sunni Islamic state ruled by Sharia law – meaning that it is extremely difficult for a conventional army to launch a counter-attack. "ISIL is not a state where you can hit military bases and infrastructure," said Hussam al-Marie, the Free Syrian Army spokesman for northern Syria. "They are just thugs, groups spread over the east of Syria and the desert."

Instead, military analysts suggest targeting their supply convoys, which travel by road through the desert. The convoys use artillery, tanks and Humvees in big convoys so would be easy to identify. Key flashpoints at the moment are the towns of Marea and Azaz, north east of Aleppo, where both Syrian government forces and ISIL are fighting to take control of the valuable resupply corridor into Syria's second city. Marea is a stronghold of the Islamic Front, a coalition of Islamist groups that is among those fighting against ISIL.

Azaz sits next to the border crossing with Turkey, which would be a valuable asset for the jihadists, and in the past few weeks the fighters have taken control of a string of villager near the two towns. Their infrastructure targets are thought to include the Haditha dam in northwestern Iraq on the Euphrates River and sections of the 600,000 barrel-a-day pipeline running to Turkey, which hasn't operated since March. The North Fertiliser Plant in Baiji, 130 miles north of Baghdad, which a Texan company won a contract to revamp in 2011, could also fall under their control – as could cement plants in the north. And once they control an area, they are careful not to repeat the mistakes made by its predecessor, the al-Qaeda-linked Islamic State of Iraq (ISI), in 2003.

Then, ISI seized control of several cities in Iraq as it fought the allied invasion, but it quickly lost them again when locals rebelled against them because their practices were too extreme. This time ISIL has been seeking to win hearts and minds. In the territory it controls, it has been quick to eradicate policies and practices that locals most hated when they were under Baghdad's rule. In Mosul, for example, corruption in public offices and financial institutions was rife. ISIL has since cracked down on officials taking bribes to do their jobs and hired an "army of accountants" to monitor the financial accounts of banks and ensure they are not embezzling funds.

Military Might

ISIL is thought to have between 7-12,000 fighters, of whom 3,000 are foreign. A quarter of those are estimated to be British, although Belgium is the largest per-capita European "source" of fighters. The extremist jihadists are using tanks, howitzers, and armoured personnel carriers seized from Iraqi arms depots in new offensives to wipe out the government's last outposts in north eastern Syria. Weapons seized from Iraq, many originally provided by the US, are now changing the dynamic of the three-year-old struggle in Syria, according to the report by IHS Country Risk.

Experts estimate ISIL has about 30 Soviet T-55 tanks and five to 10 Soviet T-72 battle tanks. They have medium-sized towed artillery pieces, with a range of upwards of 14 miles; SA-7 surface-to-air missiles; BM-21 Grad multiple rocket launchers, and Fim-92 Stinger Manpad shoulder-fired infrared homing surface-to-air missiles. Defences include ZU-23-2 anti-aircraft guns and M79 Osa, HJ-8 and AT-4 Spigot anti-tank weapons. Some think they also have a small number of helicopters. And every fighter reportedly has three sets of M16 rifles and body armour, captured from Syrian and Iraqi government forces.

Leadership

ISIL is run like a terrorist bureaucracy, with Abu Bakr al-Baghdadi, the self-proclaimed Caliph, at its head. Born in Samarra, Baghdadi was studying at the University of Islamic Sciences in Baghdad when the US invaded Iraq in March 2003. He was not thought to be connected to either al-Qaeda or its local offshoot in the early years of resistance. But by late 2005 he had been captured as a suspected mid-ranking figure in the anti-US Sunni insurgency, and he later rose to lead al-Qaeda in Iraq before splitting with them to form ISIL. He has since established a team of obedient Islamist mandarins – everything from prisoner management to suicide operations is delegated to his deputies. "He is rational," said Hisham al-Hashimi, a senior Iraqi researcher senior on Islamic militancy "He thinks very clearly about what he is doing. He is deeply ideological and committed. He is also very determined to make himself into the one true ruler of Sunni Islam." At the top is a "cabinet" of experienced military officers.

Abu Ali al-Anbari was a major general in the Iraqi military under Saddam Hussein. Under Baghdadi he is now charged with managing the Syrian territories currently under ISIL control. Another former officer from Saddam's army is Abu Muslim al-Turkmani, who was a lieutenant colonel in military intelligence. The finances of the group's Iraqi provinces are managed by a man calling himself Abu Salah. Details of the ISIL leadership structure were unearthed after documents were captured during a raid on the group's positions in June. They revealed that a series of other deputies have been assigned to a variety of roles befitting a major terrorist organisation – including the oversight of improvised explosive devices (IEDs) and caring for the families of "martyrs".

Beneath the "cabinet" level there are reportedly approximately 1,000 medium and top-level field commanders. Salaries reportedly range from $300 to $2000 per month depending on the job post.

ISIS DECLARES ITS TERRITORIES A NEW ISLAMIC STATE WITH 'RESTORATION OF CALIPHATE' IN MIDDLE EAST

The announcement will see ISIS now simply refer to itself as The Islamic State, and the group has called on al-Qa'ida and other related militant Sunni factions operating in the region to immediately pledge their allegiance. According to ISIS's chief spokesman Abu Mohammed al-Adnani, the declaration of the "restoration of the caliphate" was made after a meeting of the group's Shura Council. In recent weeks, ISIS has captured large areas of western and northern Iraq and for two years has held parts of Syria, imposing a harsh interpretation of Islamic law and in many cases, killing large numbers of opposition Shia Muslims.

Adnani said all jihadist organisations must now offer up their support to ISIS leader Abu Bakr al-Baghdadi, who has been declared Caliph of the new state. Charles Lister, visiting fellow at the Qatar-based Brookings Doha Centre, said that the declaration signalled "massive trouble" regardless of the perceived legitimacy of the ISIS group, adding that the next 24 hours will be "key". Charlie Cooper, a researcher for the Quilliam counter-extremism think-tank, said the fact Baghdadi has been named Caliph was particularly controversial.

He told *The Independent*: "There hasn't been a Caliph since the Ottoman Empire outside of the Ahmadiyya sect of Islam, and the Caliph is appointed as the only legitimate successor to Prophet Mohammed." "The fact that ISIS has done this has huge ideological and theological implications and it is a big challenge to al-Qa'ida, their spokespeople may well try to reclaim their legitimacy."

In the latest example of ISIS' sophisticated use of social media, Cooper said a new propaganda video released 15 minutes before the announcement included a "hint" towards what was about to come, with a Chilean foreign fighter describing Baghdadi as his "Caliph". "Everything that ISIS has done has been very tactical with meticulous in planning," he said. "There will be a lot of criticism from people saying announcing the restoration of the caliphate is premature, but ISIS have rapidly evolved over the past few years and there's now a cult of personality about Baghdadi in Arabic social media. "He is a very popular figure, and this will make people from al-Qa'ida and other groups question whether they should really be fighting for him."

The news came as the Iraqi army was reportedly pushed back by rebel fighters protecting insurgent positions in the northern city of Tikrit today. The military began its attempt to win back control of the city on Saturday, with a multi-pronged assault spearheaded by ground troops backed by tanks and helicopters. Security officials said the army was coordinating the campaign with the US, but reports from the ground suggested it had been forced to pull back to the town of Dijla, 25km to the south, after a failed assault in which both sides suffered casualties. The five Russian Su-25 planes are expected to enter service in the next three to four days, with more of the planes understood to be arriving soon.

Iraqi air force commander Anwar Hama Amin said the military is "in urgent need of this type of aircraft during this difficult time". Iraq's Prime Minister Nouri Maliki has blamed much of the rebels success on the Iraqi military's lack of air support. The country signed contracts to buy F-16 jets from the USA, but has been slow in receiving them. He said Iraq is also hoping to acquire second-hand fighter jets from Belarus. The deals are together thought to be worth about $500 million (£293m). The UN says that more than 1,000 people, largely civilians, have been killed in fighting between Iraqi forces and the rebels.

The US has now deployed drones to the region around Tikrit, Saddam Hussein's home town, though the White House said it has not yet authorised air strikes against militants and the drones will only be used for 'force protection'. Other countries including Iran are thought to have stationed military equipment and forces in the region. Professor Peter Neumann, of the International Centre for the Study of Radicalisation at King's College London, said the significance of the announcement should not be underestimated. "It's a declaration of war - not only against the West and all the countries that are currently fighting ISIS but, more importantly, against al-Qa'ida.

ISIS now see themselves as the legitimate leaders of the movement and they expect everyone to fall in line. "For ideological jihadists, the caliphate is the ultimate aim, and ISIS - in their eyes - have come closer to realising that vision than anyone else. On that basis, ISIS leaders believe they deserve everyone's allegiance. "This could be the end of al-Qa'ida. It depends on how al-Qa'ida will respond. Unless they come out fighting, this could mark the end of [Osama] Bin Laden's vision and his legacy."

Prof Neumann said the declaration of a caliphate showed how confident ISIS was after making spectacular gains in Iraq in recent weeks. "They haven't lost any of the momentum they gained when capturing Mosul," he said. "On the contrary, they've held on to it, gained more territory and have seen jihadists from other groups swear allegiance to ISIS. "They must think their dream of creating the caliphate is finally coming true, and it's coming true faster and more dramatically than even they expected."

ISIS SPOKESMAN DECLARES CALIPHATE, REBRANDS GROUP AS "ISLAMIC STATE"

Abu Muhammad al-'Adnani, the official spokesman of the Islamic State in Iraq and Sham (ISIS), announced the group's rebranding as the "Islamic State," declaring itself a Caliphate and its leader, Abu Bakr al-Baghdadi, the Caliph Ibrahim.

His announcement came in a 34 minute speech entitled, "This is the Promise of Allah," and was posted on the Twitter account of the group's al-I'tisaam Media Foundation. Concurrently, the Islamic State's al-Hayat Media Center provided English, French, German, and Russian translations. In the speech, 'Adnani demanded that all jihadi factions, not only those in Iraq and Syria, but everywhere, pledge allegiance to the Islamic State, for the "legality" of their organizations is now void. He stated: "Indeed, it is the State. Indeed, it is the khilâfah. It is time for you to end this abhorrent partisanship, dispersion, and division, for this condition is not from the religion of Allah at all. And if you forsake the State or wage war against it, you will not harm it. You will only harm yourselves." 'Adnani also acknowledged Abu Bakr al-Baghdadi by his real name and lineage, Ibrâhîm Ibn 'Awwâd Ibn Ibrâhîm Ibn 'Alî Ibn Muhammad al-Badrî al-Hâshimî al-Husaynî al-Qurashî, and declared him the Caliph for Muslims everywhere.

Following is a copy of the English translation:

THIS IS THE PROMISE OF ALLAH

Praise be to Allah, the Mighty and Strong. And may peace and blessings be upon the one sent with the sword as a mercy to all creation. As for what follows: Allah (the Exalted) said: {Allah has promised those who have believed among you and done righteous deeds that He will surely grant them succession [to authority] upon the earth just as He granted it to those before them and that He will surely establish for them their religion which He has preferred for them and that He will surely substitute for them, after their fear, security, [for] they worship Me, not associating anything with Me. But whoever disbelieves after that – then those are the defiantly disobedient} [An-Nûr:55].

Succession, establishment, and safety – a promise from Allah reserved for the Muslims, but with a condition. {They worship me [Allah] and do not associate anything with me} [An-Nûr: 55]. Having faith in Allah, keeping far from the gateways to shirk (polytheism) and its various shades, along with submitting to Allah's command in everything big and small, and giving Him the level of obedience that makes your lusts, inclinations, and desires to be in compliance with what the Prophet (peace be upon him) came with – only after this condition is met will the promise be fulfilled. For by fulfilling this condition comes the ability to build, reform, remove oppression, spread justice, and bring about safety and tranquility. Only by meeting this condition, will there be the succession, which Allah informed the angels about.

Without this condition being met, authority becomes nothing more than kingship, dominance and rule, accompanied with destruction, corruption, oppression, subjugation, fear, and the decadence of the human being and his descent to the level of animals. That is the reality of succession, which Allah created us for. It is not simply kingship, subjugation, dominance, and rule. Rather, succession is to utilize all that for the purpose of compelling the people to do what the Sharia (Allah's law) requires of them concerning their interests in the hereafter and worldly life, which can only be achieved by carrying out the command of Allah, establishing His religion, and referring to His law for judgment.

This succession, along with the aforementioned reality, is the purpose for which Allah sent His messengers and revealed His scriptures, and for which the swords of jihad were unsheathed.

Indeed, Allah (the Exalted) honored the ummah (nation) of Muhammad and blessed them. He made them the best ummah of all peoples.

{You are the best nation produced [as an example] for mankind. You enjoin what is right and forbid what is wrong and believe in Allah} [Âl 'Imrân: 110].

And He promised to grant the ummah succession to authority. {Allah has promised those who have believed among you and done righteous deeds that He will surely grant them succession [to authority] upon the earth just as He granted it to those before them} [An-Nûr: 55].

He also made leadership of the world and mastership of the earth for the ummah, as long as it fulfilled the condition: {They worship me [Allah] and do not associate anything with me} [An-Nûr: 55].

Allah (the Exalted) also gave honor to the ummah. {And to Allah belongs [all] honor, and to His Messenger, and to the believers, but the hypocrites do not know} [Al-Munâfiqûn: 8].

Yes, honor is for this ummah. It is from the honor of Allah (the Exalted) – honor that mixes with the faith residing in the believer's heart. Thus, if faith becomes firm in the heart, honor becomes firm along with it. It is honor that does not hunch, soften, or become disgraced regardless of how great the anguish and tribulation become. It is honor befitting the best ummah – the ummah of Muhammad (peace be upon him) – an ummah that does not accept submission to anyone or anything other than Allah. It does not accept transgression nor oppression. {And those who, when tyranny strikes them, they defend themselves} [Ash-Shûrâ: 39].

This is an honorable and noble ummah, which does not sleep and ignore grievance. It does not accept degradation. {So do not weaken and do not grieve, and you will be superior if you are [true] believers} [Âl 'Imrân:139].

It is a mighty and powerful ummah. How can it not be such, when Allah supports it and grants it victory? {That is because Allah is the protector of those who have believed and because the disbelievers have no protector} [Muhammad: 11].

This is the ummah of Muhammad (peace be upon him) which, whenever it is truthful with Allah, He brings about His promise for them. Allah (the Exalted) sent His Prophet (peace be upon him), while the Arabs were in the depths of ignorance and blinding darkness. They were the most naked, the hungriest, and the most backwards of peoples, sinking in depths of lowness. No one cared about them or gave them any regard. They submitted in humiliation to Khosrau and Caesar, yielding to the conqueror.

Allah (the Exalted) said, {Although they were before in clear error} [Al-Jumu'ah: 2]. Allah (the Exalted) also said, {And remember when you were few and oppressed in the land, fearing that people might abduct you} [Al-Anfâl: 26].

Qatâdah (may Allah have mercy upon him) said in explanation of this verse, "These clans of Arabs were the most disgraced, the hungriest, the most ignorant, and the most naked. They were people who were eaten but did not eat. Whoever lived from them lived miserably. And whoever died from them fell into hellfire." His words end here, may Allah have mercy upon him.

A group of the Sahâbah (companions of the Prophet – peace be upon him) entered upon Khosrau Yazdajard on the day of the battle of al-Qâdisiyyah to call him to Islam. He said to them, "I don't know any nation on the earth that was more miserable, fewer in number, and more divided than you. We would entrust the people of the villages in the outskirts to hold you back. Persia did not wage war against you, nor did you ever hope to stand and face it." So they were silenced. Then al-Mughîrah Ibn Shu'bah (may Allah be pleased with him) responded to him, saying, "As for what you've mentioned of our poor condition, then there was no condition poorer than ours. As for our hunger, then it was unlike any hunger. We used to eat scarabs, beetles, scorpions, and snakes. We considered such as food. As for our homes, then they were nothing but the surface of the earth. We did not use to wear anything except what we made from the fur of our camels and sheep. Our religion was to kill each other and oppress each other. One of us would bury his daughter alive, hating the thought that she would eat from his food."

This was the condition of the Arabs before Islam. They were in dispute and broken up; they were dispersed and had infighting, striking each other's necks, suffering hunger, lack of unity, and capture. Then, when Allah blessed them with Islam and they believed, Allah unified them, united their ranks, honored them after their humiliation, enriched them after their poverty, and brought their hearts together, all through Islam. Thus, by the grace of Allah, they became brothers.

Allah (the Exalted) said, {And He brought together their hearts. If you had spent all that is in the earth, you could not have brought their hearts together; but Allah brought them together} [Al-Anfâl: 63].

So the animosity and hatred they had for each other vanished from their hearts. They were united by faith, and piety became their measuring scale. They did not differentiate between an Arab and a non-Arab, nor between an easterner and a westerner, nor between a white person and a black person, nor between a poor person and a rich person. They abandoned nationalism and the calls of jâhiliyyah (pre-Islamic ignorance), raised the flag of lâ ilâha ill Allâh (there is no god but Allah) and carried out jihad in the path of Allah with truthfulness and sincerity. So Allah raised them through this religion and honored them by having them carry its message. He bestowed His grace on them, and made them the kings and masters of the world.

Our dear ummah – the best of peoples – Allah (the Exalted) decrees numerous victories for this ummah to occur in a single year, which He does not grant others in many years or even centuries. This ummah succeeded in ending two of the largest empires known to history in just 25 years, and then spent the treasures of those empires on jihad in the path of Allah. They put out the fire of the Magians (fireworshippers) forever, and they forced the noses of the cross-worshippers onto the ground with the most miserable of weapons and weakest of numbers. Ibn Abî Shaybah reported in "al-Musannaf" that Husayn reported that Abû Wâ'il said that when Sa'd Ibn Abî Waqqas had arrived and rested at al-Qâdisiyyah with the people, he said, "I'm not sure if we were more than 7 or 8 thousand or so. The mushrikîn (polytheists) were about 60 thousand or so. They had elephants with them. When they arrived, they said to us, 'Go back [to your land], because we don't see with you any numbers, strength, or arms. So go back.' We answered them saying, 'We will not go back.' Then they started mocking our arrows saying, 'Dûk, dûk,' [a Persian word] comparing our arrows to spindles."

Yes, my ummah, those barefoot, naked, shepherds who did not know good from evil, nor truth from falsehood, filled the earth with justice after it had been filled with oppression and tyranny, and ruled the world for centuries. This was neither through any means of strength that they possessed or numbers that they commanded, nor through their wisdom but rather, through their faith in Allah (the Exalted) and their adherence to the guidance of His Messenger (peace be upon him). O ummah of Muhammad (peace be upon him), you continue to be the best ummah and continue to have honor. Leadership will return to you. The God of this ummah yesterday is the same God of the ummah today, and the One who gave it victory yesterday is the One who will give it victory today.

The time has come for those generations that were drowning in oceans of disgrace, being nursed on the milk of humiliation, and being ruled by the vilest of all people, after their long slumber in the darkness of neglect – the time has come for them to rise. The time has come for the ummah of Muhammad (peace be upon him) to wake up from its sleep, remove the garments of dishonor, and shake off the dust of humiliation and disgrace, for the era of lamenting and moaning has gone, and the dawn of honor has emerged anew. The sun of jihad has risen. The glad tidings of good are shining. Triumph looms on the horizon. The signs of victory have appeared.

Here the flag of the Islamic State, the flag of tawhîd (monotheism), rises and flutters. Its shade covers land from Aleppo to Diyala. Beneath it, the walls of the tawâghît (rulers claiming the rights of Allah) have been demolished, their flags have fallen, and their borders have been destroyed.

Their soldiers are either killed, imprisoned, or defeated. The Muslims are honored. The kuffâr (infidels) are disgraced. Ahlus-Sunnah (the Sunnis) are masters and are esteemed. The people of bid'ah (heresy) are humiliated. The hudûd (Sharia penalties) are implemented – the hudûd of Allah – all of them. The frontlines are defended.

Crosses and graves are demolished. Prisoners are released by the edge of the sword. The people in the lands of the State move about for their livelihood and journeys, feeling safe regarding their lives and wealth. Wulât (plural of wâlî or "governors") and judges have been appointed. Jizyah (a tax imposed on kuffâr) has been enforced.

Fay' (money taken from the kuffâr without battle) and zakat (obligatory alms) have been collected. Courts have been established to resolve disputes and complaints. Evil has been removed. Lessons and classes have been held in the masâjid (plural of masjid) and, by the grace of Allah, the religion has become completely for Allah. There only remained one matter, a wâjib kifâ'î (collective obligation) that the ummah sins by abandoning. It is a forgotten obligation. The ummah has not tasted honor since they lost it. It is a dream that lives in the depths of every Muslim believer. It is a hope that flutters in the heart of every mujâhid muwahhid (monotheist). It is the khilâfah (caliphate). It is the khilâfah – the abandoned obligation of the era.

Allah (the Exalted) said, {And mention when your Lord said to the angels, "Indeed, I will make upon the earth a khalîfah"} [Al-Baqarah: 30].

Imam al-Qurtubî said in his tafsîr (Quranic exegesis), "This verse is a fundamental basis for the appointment of a leader and khalîfah (caliph) who is listened to and obeyed so that the ummah is united by him and his orders are carried out. There is no dispute over this matter between the ummah nor between the scholars, except for what has been reported from al-Asamm [the meaning of his name is "the deaf man"], for his deafness prevented him from hearing the Sharia." That ends his words, may Allah have mercy upon him.

Therefore, the shûrâ (consultation) council of the Islamic State studied this matter after the Islamic State – by Allah's grace – gained the essentials necessary for khilâfah, which the Muslims are sinful for if they do not try to establish. In light of the fact that the Islamic State has no shar'î (legal) constraint or excuse that can justify delaying or neglecting the establishment of the khilâfah such that it would not be sinful, the Islamic State – represented by ahlul-halli-wal-'aqd (its people of authority), consisting of its senior figures, leaders, and the shûrâ council – resolved to announce the establishment of the Islamic khilâfah, the appointment of a khalîfah for the Muslims, and the pledge of allegiance to the shaykh (sheikh), the mujâhid, the scholar who practices what he preaches, the worshipper, the leader, the warrior, the reviver, descendent from the family of the Prophet, the slave of Allah, Ibrâhîm Ibn 'Awwâd Ibn Ibrâhîm Ibn 'Alî Ibn Muhammad al-Badrî al-Hâshimî al-Husaynî al-Qurashî by lineage, as-Sâmurrâ'î by birth and upbringing, al-Baghdâdî by residence and scholarship. And he has accepted the bay'ah (pledge of allegiance). Thus, he is the imam and khalîfah for the Muslims everywhere. Accordingly, the "Iraq and Shâm" in the name of the Islamic State is henceforth removed from all official deliberations and communications, and the official name is the Islamic State from the date of this declaration.

We clarify to the Muslims that with this declaration of khilâfah, it is incumbent upon all Muslims to pledge allegiance to the khalîfah Ibrâhîm and support him (may Allah preserve him). The legality of all emirates, groups, states, and organizations, becomes null by the expansion of the khilâfah's authority and arrival of its troops to their areas. Imam Ahmad (may Allah have mercy upon him) said, as reported by 'Abdûs Ibn Mâlik al-'Attâr, "It is not permissible for anyone who believes in Allah to sleep without considering as his leader whoever conquers them by the sword until he becomes khalîfah and is called Amîrul-Mu'minîn (the leader of the believers), whether this leader is righteous or sinful."

The khalîfah Ibrâhîm (may Allah preserve him) has fulfilled all the conditions for khilâfah mentioned by the scholars. He was given bay'ah in Iraq by the people of authority in the Islamic State as the successor to Abû 'Umar al-Baghdâdî (may Allah have mercy upon him). His authority has expanded over wide areas in Iraq and Shâm.

The land now submits to his order and authority from Aleppo to Diyala. So fear Allah, O slaves of Allah. Listen to your khalîfah and obey him. Support your state, which grows everyday – by Allah's grace – with honor and loftiness, while its enemy increases in retreat and defeat.

So rush O Muslims and gather around your khalîfah, so that you may return as you once were for ages, kings of the earth and knights of war. Come so that you may be honored and esteemed, living as masters with dignity. Know that we fight over a religion that Allah promised to support. We fight for an ummah to which Allah has given honor, esteem, and leadership, promising it with empowerment and strength on the earth. Come O Muslims to your honor, to your victory. By Allah, if you disbelieve in democracy, secularism, nationalism, as well as all the other garbage and ideas from the west, and rush to your religion and creed, then by Allah, you will own the earth, and the east and west will submit to you. This is the promise of Allah to you. This is the promise of Allah to you. {So do not weaken and do not grieve, and you will be superior if you are believers} [Âl 'Imrân: 139].

This is the promise of Allah to you. {If Allah should aid you, no one can overcome you} [Âl 'Imrân: 160].

This is the promise of Allah to you. {So do not weaken and call for peace while you are superior; and Allah is with you and will never deprive you of [the reward of] your deeds} [Muhammad: 35].

This is the promise of Allah to you. {Allah has promised those who have believed among you and done righteous deeds that He will surely grant them succession [to authority] upon the earth just as He granted it to those before them and that He will surely establish for them [therein] their religion which He has preferred for them} [An-Nûr: 55].

So come to the promise of your Lord. {Indeed, Allah does not fail in His promise} [Âl 'Imrân: 9]

And a message to all the platoons and groups on the face of the earth, consisting of mujahidin and people working to support the religion of Allah and raising the Islamic banners – a message to the heads and leaders of these groups – we say:

Fear Allah with regards to yourselves. Fear Allah with regards to your jihad. Fear Allah with regards to your ummah. {O you who have believed, fear Allah as He should be feared and do not die except as Muslims, and hold firmly to the rope of Allah all together and do not become divided.} [Âl 'Imrân: 102-103].

We – by Allah – do not find any shar'î (legal) excuse for you justifying your holding back from supporting this state. Take a stance on account of which Allah (the Exalted) will be pleased with you. The veil has been lifted and the truth has become clear. Indeed, it is the State. It is the state for the Muslims – the oppressed of them, the orphans, the widows, and the impoverished. If you support it, then you do so for your own good.

Indeed, it is the State. Indeed, it is the khilâfah. It is time for you to end this abhorrent partisanship, dispersion, and division, for this condition is not from the religion of Allah at all. And if you forsake the State or wage war against it, you will not harm it. You will only harm yourselves. It is the State – the state for the Muslims. Sufficient for you should be what al-Bukhârî (may Allah have mercy upon him) reported from Mu'âwiyah (may Allah be pleased with him). He said that he heard Allah's Messenger (peace be upon him) say, "This matter is for Quraysh. No one opposes them regarding it except that Allah throws him down on his face, as lông as they establish the religion." As for you, O soldiers of the platoons and organizations, know that after this consolidation and the establishment of the khilâfah, the legality of your groups and organizations has become invalid. It is not permissible for a single person of you who believes in Allah to sleep without having walâ' (loyalty) to the khalîfah. If your leaders whisper to you claiming it is not a khilâfah, then remember how long they whispered to you claiming that it was not a state but rather a fictional, cardboard entity, until its certain news reached you. It is a state. Its news will continue to reach you showing that it is a khilâfah, even if after time.

And know that nothing has delayed victory and delays it now more than these organizations, because they are the cause of division and disagreements that ruin strength. Division is not from Islam at all. {Indeed, those who have divided their religion and become sects – you are not [associated] with them in anything. Their affair is only [left] to Allah; then He will inform them about what they used to do} [Al-An'âm: 159].

{[Adhere to the religion], turning in repentance to Him, and fear Him and establish prayer and do not be of those who associate others with Allah, of those who have divided their religion and become sects, every faction rejoicing in what it has.} [Ar-Rûm: 31-32]

Know that your leaders will not find any arguments to keep you away from the jamâ'ah (the body of Muslims united behind a Muslim leader), the khilâfah, and this great good, except for two false and weak excuses. The first excuse is the same matter they have accused it with before, that it is a state of khawârij (a sect that excommunicated Muslims for sins that do not warrant excommunication) and other accusations whose falseness has become apparent in the cities that are ruled by the State. Second, your leaders will assure both you and themselves saying, "This is just a gust of wind which will be extinguished, or a temporary whirlwind that will not last, and that the nations of kufr (disbelief) won't allow it to remain, and they will gather against it so that it disappears quickly and soon. Those of its soldiers who survive will end up in mountaintops, caverns, deserts, and clandestine prisons. Thereafter we will have to return to the jihad of the elite. We cannot handle jihad of the elite far away from hotels, conferences, offices, lights, and cameras. We want to lead the ummah in the jihad of the ummah..."

So let those leaders be ruined. And let that "ummah" they want to unite be ruined – an "ummah" of secularists, democrats, and nationalists... an "ummah" of murji'ah (a sect that excludes deeds from faith), ikhwân (the "Muslim Brotherhood" party), and surûriyyah (a sect influenced by the ikhwân claiming to be Salafî). {Satan promises them and arouses desire in them. But Satan does not promise them except delusion} [An-Nisâ': 120].

The State will remain, by Allah's permission. Ask the parties in Iraq and their leaders. How much did they reassure themselves by claiming that the state would vanish. They were greater than your parties in power and greater in accumulation of wealth. {Have they not traveled through the earth and observed how was the end of those before them? They were greater than them in power} [Ar-Rûm: 9]

As for you, O soldiers of the Islamic State, then congratulations to you. Congratulations on this clear victory, congratulations on this great triumph. Today the kâfirîn (infidels) are infuriated in such a manner after which there will be no similar infuriation. Many of them almost die from anger and sorrow. Today the believers rejoice with victory from Allah, feeling great happiness. Today the hypocrites are degraded. Today the râfidah (shia), sahwât (awakening councils), and murtaddîn (apostates) are humiliated.

Today the tawâghît in the east and west are frightened. Today the nations of kufr in the west are terrified. Today the flags of Shaytân (Satan) and his party have fallen. Today the flag of tawhîd rises with its people. Today the Muslims are honored. Today the Muslims are honored. Now the khilâfah has returned, humbling the necks of the enemy. Now the khilâfah has returned in spite of its opponents. Now the khilâfah has returned; we ask Allah (the Exalted) to make it to be upon the methodology of prophethood. Now hope is being actualized. Now the dream has become a reality. Congratulations to you. You spoke and were truthful. You promised and kept to your word.

O soldiers of the Islamic State, it is from the great blessings of Allah upon you that He allowed you to reach this day and witness this victory, which did not arrive except by the grace of Allah (the Exalted) and then by the blood and corpses of thousands of your brothers who preceded you from the best of mankind. We consider them such and Allah is their judge, and we do not presume to know better than Him. They are those who carried this banner and under it sacrificed everything. They offered everything generously, even their souls, to pass on this great banner to you. Indeed, they did so. May Allah have mercy upon them and reward them with every good on behalf of Islam. So protect this great trust. Raise this banner with strength. Water it with your blood. Raise it upon your corpses. Die under it, until you pass it on – if Allah wills – to 'Îsâ (Jesus) the son of Maryam (Mary), peace be upon him.

O soldiers of the Islamic State, Allah (the Exalted) ordered us with jihad and promised us with victory but He did not make us responsible for victory. Indeed, Allah (the Exalted) blessed you today with this victory, thus we announced the khilâfah in compliance with the order of Allah (the Exalted). We announced it because – by Allah's grace – we have its essentials. By Allah's permission, we are capable of establishing the khilâfah. So we carry out the order of Allah (the Exalted) and we are justified – if Allah wills – and we do not care thereafter what happens, even if we only remain for one day or one hour, and to Allah belongs the matter before and after. If Allah (the Exalted) causes the khilâfah to remain and gain strength, then such is by His grace and bounty alone, for victory is only from Him. And if it vanishes and weakens, then know that such is from ourselves and because of our deeds.

We will defend it – if Allah wills – as long as it exists and as long as one of us remains, and [if it vanishes]

We will bring it back – if Allah wills – upon the methodology of prophethood.

Whoever has the loftiest height as his own ambition,

Then everything he faces will be beloved. [Poetry]

O soldiers of the Islamic State, you will be facing malâhim (fierce battles) that cause the children's hair to become grey. You will be facing fitan (tribulations) and hardships of many different colors. You will be facing tests and quakes. No one will survive them except he whom Allah grants mercy. No one will be firm during these fitan except one whom Allah keeps firm. The worst of these fitan is that of the dunyâ (worldly life). So be wary of competing over it. Be wary. Remember the greatest responsibility that is now on your backs. You are now the defenders of the land of Islam and its guards. You will not be able to preserve this trust and defend this land, except by fearing Allah secretly and publically, then by sacrificing, being patient, and offering blood.

I am amazed by those who possess the stature of men and the sharpness of arrows,

Yet their command is not made nor executed.

I am amazed by those who find the path to lofty heights,

Yet do not traverse the path, wearing it down until no mounds are left.

And I have not found a fault in people like that of those

Who are capable of completing their effort, but instead abort it. [Poetry]

Also know that one of the biggest factors that brought about this victory that Allah (the Exalted) has blessed you with is your support of each other, the absence of disagreement, your listening to and obedience of your leaders, and your patience with them. So keep this factor in mind and preserve it. Unite with each other and do not disagree with each other. Accept each other and do not argue with each other. Be very wary of breaking the ranks. For you to be snatched by birds would be better for you than to break the ranks or take part in doing so. And if anyone wants to break the ranks, split his head with bullets and empty its insides, whoever he may be.

The Messenger of Allah (peace be upon him) said: "And whoever pledges allegiance to a leader giving his hand in oath with the sincerity of his heart, then he must obey him when he can. If someone else comes and tries to dispute with the leader [over leadership] then strike the neck of the latter." This was reported by Muslim.

On the authority of Abdullâh Ibn 'Amr (may Allah be pleased with them both) and Abû Hurayrah (may Allah be pleased with him), who reported that the Messenger of Allah (peace be upon him) said: "Whoever obeys me has obeyed Allah, and whoever disobeys me has disobeyed Allah. Whoever obeys the leader has obeyed me, and whoever disobeys the leader has disobeyed me. Indeed the leader is a shield. Behind him fighting is carried out, and by him [the people] are defended. So if he orders the people to fear Allah and he is just, then he is rewarded. And if he orders with anything else, then he will be held accountable for that." This was reported by al-Bukhârî.

O soldiers of the Islamic State, there is one more matter that I wish to call your attention to. They will look for something to criticize and will attempt to raise misconceptions.

So if they ask you, "How can you announce the khilâfah when the ummah has not rallied behind you? For your authority is not accepted by the groups, factions, detachments, brigades, corps, banners, sects, parties, assemblies, councils, institutions, coordination teams, leagues, coalitions, armies, fronts, movements, and organizations." Then say to them, {But they will not cease to differ except whom your Lord has given mercy} [Hûd: 118-119].

They have never united on a single issue, nor will they ever unite on any issue except for those whom Allah has mercy upon. Furthermore, the Islamic State will bring together those who want unity.

If they tell you, "You have stepped over them and acted on your own judgment. Why did you not consult the other groups, pardon them, and tolerate them?" Then say to them, "The issue is too urgent." {And I hastened to You, my Lord, that You be pleased} [Tâhâ: 84].

And say to them, "Whom would we consult? They never recognized the Islamic State to begin with, although America, Britain and France acknowledge its existence. Whom would we consult? Should we consult those who have abandoned us? Those who have betrayed us? Those who have disowned us and incited against us? Those who have become hostile towards us? Those who wage war against us? Whom would we consult, and whom did we step over?"

Indeed the difference between me and my brothers and cousins is very big. They do not come to my aid, but if they called me for help I would come to their rescue. [Poetry]

And if they tell you, "We do not accept your authority". Then say to them, "We had the ability to establish the khilâfah, by the grace of Allah, so it became an obligation for us to do so. Therefore, we hastened in adherence to the command of Allah (the Exalted):

{It is not for a believing man or a believing woman, when Allah and His Messenger have decided a matter,

that they should [thereafter] have any choice about their affair} [Al-Ahzâb: 36].

And say to them, "We spilled rivers of our blood to water the seeds of the khilâfah, laid its foundation with our skulls, and built its tower over our corpses. We were patient for years in the face of being killed, imprisoned, having our bones broken and our limbs severed. We drank all sorts of bitterness, dreaming of this day. Would we delay it for even a moment after having reached it?"

And say to them,

We took it forcibly at the point of a blade.

We brought it back conquered and compelled.

We established it in defiance of many.

And the people's necks were violently struck,

With bombings, explosions, and destruction,

And soldiers that do not see hardship as being difficult,

And lions that are thirsty in battle,

Having greedily drunk the blood of kufr.

Our khilâfah has indeed returned with certainty

And likewise our state, becoming a firm structure.

And the breasts of the believers have been healed,

While the hearts of kufr have been filled with terror. [Poetry]

In conclusion, we congratulate the Muslims on the advent of the blessed month of Ramadan. We ask Allah (the Exalted) to make it a month of victory, honor, and consolidation for the Muslims, and make its days and its nights a curse for the râfidah, the sahwât, and the murtaddîn. {And Allah is predominant over His affair, but most of the people do not know.} [Yûsuf: 21]

MUJAHIDEEN SHURA COUNCIL (IRAQ)

The Mujahideen Shura Council was an umbrella organization of at least six SunniIslamist groups taking part in the Iraqi insurgency: al-Qaeda in Iraq (*Tenzheem Qa'adah al-Jihad*), *Jeish al-Taiifa al-Mansoura, Katbiyan Ansar Al-Tawhid wal Sunnah,* Saray al-Jihad Group, al-Ghuraba Brigades, and al-Ahwal Brigades.

The formation of the group was first announced on January 15, 2006, in a statement posted to the jihadist website Hanin Net. The statement was signed by the spokesman for Tenzheem Qa'adah al-Jihad, Abu Maysarah al-Iraqi. It was formed to resist efforts by the American and Iraqi authorities to win over Sunni supporters of the insurgency. The stated purpose of the council was "Managing the struggle in the battle of confrontation to ward off the invading *kafir* (infidels) and their apostate stooges...Uniting the word of the*mujahideen* and closing their ranks...[and] determining a clear position toward developments and incidents so that people can see things clearly and the truth will not be confused with falsehood." On or before April 25, 2006, a videotape of Abu Musab al-Zarqawi was released bearing the organization's logo. The Mujahideen Shura Council was believed by the United States Marine Corps to be the primary political force in the Al Anbar province. The group was headed by Abdullah Rashid al-Baghdadi (*nom de guerre*: Abu Omar al-Baghdadi). In mid-October 2006, a statement was released, stating that the Mujahideen Shura Council had been disbanded, and was replaced by the Islamic State of Iraq.

History

Formation

On January 15, 2006, a spokesman of al Qaeda in Iraq, announced the formation of the "Majlis Shura al-Mujahideen fi al-

Iraq" (Mujahideen Shura Council in Iraq or Mujaheddin Consultative Council), a coalition of about six insurgent organizations. This was apparently an attempt at regaining support.

Structure

Little is known about the organizational structure of the Council, in large part due to the shadowy nature of the organization itself. al Qaeda in Iraq was the most powerful and visible group. Because of the multiple leaders the Shura Council had, there seems to have been no disruption in the Shura Council's ability to carry out attacks: more than 1600 Iraqi civilians died in the month right after Zarqawi's death, the largest number killed in a month to that date. Elements of the Shura Council's organization from the top to the bottom remain fluid due both to the nature of its aims and methods as well as its loose confederation. It was speculated that the group was dominated by al Qaeda in Iraq and that Zarqawi's death dealt a severe blow to the unity of the Council.

Aside from the murky workings of the Shura Council's leadership it is known that the Council has rather smooth operations when it comes to propaganda, the Council's propaganda czar, Murasel, regularly posted updates, criticisms, and praises for the Council's own acts of violence on a semi-daily basis at blogspot.com.

Iraqi insurgency

On June 16, 2006, the council claimed responsibility for the kidnapping of two U.S. soldiers, Private First Class Thomas Lowell Tucker and Private First Class Kristian Menchaca, during an attack that day on a roadside checkpoint in Youssifiya, an area known as the Triangle of Death. The soldiers were actually killed in the attack and their bodies were found in Youssifiyah on June 19, 2006.

On October 15, 2006, the Council released a video declaring an Islamic State of Iraq, made up of six provinces including Baghdad. The Iraqi government discounted this, noting none of the provinces mentioned were in insurgent control.

On the same day, the Ba'ath Socialist Party, released a statement which warned against 'backing any divisive plan under the pretext to protect whatever community...', a direct reference to the attempted establishment of a separate Sunni Arab state. On October 18, 2006, according to Brig. Abdul-Karim Khalaf of the Interior Ministry, about 60 al-Qaida militants arrived in Ramadi, 70 miles (110 km) west of Baghdad, in 17 vehicles and remained there for 15 minutes before being forced to flee, suffering unspecified losses in clashes with security and "tribal forces".

Witnesses said that dozens of masked militants dressed in white marched through the streets of the city, the capital of western Anbar province, carrying banners exhorting people to support the Islamic State of Iraq. "We are from Mujahideen Shura Council and our Amir (Prince) is Abu Omar al-Baghdadi. God willing we will set the law of Sharia here and we will fight the Americans," said a man who identified himself as Abu Harith. "We have announced the Islamic state. Ramadi is part of it. Our state will comprise all the Sunni provinces of Iraq".

Disbanding

In mid-October 2006, a statement was released, stating that the Mujahideen Shura Council had changed its name to the Islamic State of Iraq. Then, in November, a statement was issued by Abu Hamza al-Muhajir stating that the Mujahideen Shura Council had been disbanded, in favor of a new group under the banner of the Islamic State of Iraq. The reason given for this shift was that a new phase of jihad was beginning, in which they would attempt to reestablish the Islamic caliphate. After this statement, there were a few more claims of responsibility issued under the name of the Mujahideen Shura Council, but these eventually ceased and were totally replaced by claims from the Islamic State of Iraq.

ANALYSIS: WHAT WE TALK ABOUT WHEN WE TALK ABOUT IRAQ AND SYRIA

The first weeks of June saw a series of dramatic events unfold in Iraq. The Islamic State of Iraq and the Levant (ISIL)—the organization that evolved out of al Qaeda in Iraq (AQI)— fought alongside other militant Sunni groups to rout the Iraqi Army in Mosul and quickly continued on to Tikrit and the oil fields of Baji. At the same time, Iraqi Kurdish troops were able to seize the oil-rich city of Kirkuk without a fight. Meanwhile, in neighboring

Syria, ISIL continues to hold ground in several provinces (namely Raqqa, but with increasing gains in Hasakeh and Deir Ezzor) as it confronts both the Assad regime and other anti-Assad groups contending for power.

While Syria watchers have been focused on ISIL for some time, most did not anticipate such rapid or successful actions from the group in Iraq. As such, Caerus has received a flood of questions about the group—its origins, its ties to al-Qaeda, its current standing in both Iraq and Syria, and what the future holds. Caerus will periodically update this document with new information as events in the region unfold.

Is ISIL one Organization or Two?

It is one organization, with multiple translations and abbreviations of its name.

In Arabic:

- *Al-Dawla al-Islamiyya fi al-Iraq wa al-Sham* "'D/HD) 'D'3D'EJ) AJ 'D91'B H'D4'E" - translation: "The Islamic State in Iraq and Sham"
- *Da'esh* "/'94" – the Arabic acronym for ISIL

In English:

- The Islamic State of Iraq and the Levant (ISIL)
- The Islamic State of Iraq and Syria (ISIS)
- The Islamic State of Iraq and Sham (ISIS)

The "Levant" is a reference to the eastern Mediterranean, including the modern-day countries of Syria, Lebanon, Jordan and Palestine. Literally "rising" in French, the term refers to the east, where the sun rises. "Sham" is a term for "Greater Syria" referencing the same general geographic region as the 'Levant'. It is also used colloquially in Arabic to refer to Syria, or Damascus.

Did ISIL Change its Name Again?

ISIL now refers to itself as The Islamic State. On 29 June 2014, ISIL released a statement declaring a new caliphate with Abu Bakr al-Baghdadi as Caliph Ibrahim and "leader of Muslims everywhere." ISIL also demanded allegiance (or *bay'a*) of all active jihadi organizations, a move that puts it in direct competition with al Qaeda and its affiliated groups.

What are ISIL's Origins?

The Islamic State of Iraq and the Levant (ISIL) is the present-day incarnation of al-Qaeda in Iraq (AQI)/the Islamic State of Iraq (ISI). Distinct from Jabhat al-Nusra (JN) in Syria and no longer officially connected to al-Qaeda, ISIL seeks to build a "Caliphate" (Islamic state) in the Levant and is currently operating across Syria and Iraq.

ISIL's origins trace back to the group Jamaat al-Tawhid wal-Jihad, formed in Jordan in 2002. It was later named Tanzeem Qaedat al-Jihad fi Bilad al-Rafidayn, otherwise known as al-Qaeda in Iraq (AQI) after pledging allegiance to Osama bin Laden in 2004. In late 2005, its then leader Abu Muzab al-Zarqawi united various jihadist groups under the banner of the Mujahideen Shura Council and instilled a cult of violence that endures in the group today. After Zarqawi's death in June 2006, his successor, Abu Hamza al-Muhajer, also known as Abu Ayyub al-Masri, declared the formation of the Islamic State of Iraq (ISI), led by Abu Omar al-Baghdadi. Al-Masri and al-Baghdadi were kilied by US and Iraqi forces in Tikrit in 2010, at which point the current "Emir" of ISIL, Abu Bakr al-Baghdadi, was appointed.

Over the course of their operation, AQI/ISI alienated local Iraqi residents, resulting in catastrophic open conflict with nearly all other Iraqi tribes and militias. In what was known as the "Sahwa" (Awakening) movement, Iraqi communities cooperated with the Iraqi government and US forces to nearly destroy AQI/ISI. By the May 2011 death of Osama Bin Laden, AQI/ISI

In Iraq, the group slowly re-emerged in the years following Iraq's 2010 national elections and the withdrawal of US troops. Iraqi Prime Minister, Nouri al-Maliki, formed a government despite his bloc losing by two seats to Ayad Allawi, a Shiite politician whose bloc included most influential Sunni politicians. Allawi represented the frustrations of many Sunni communities when he complained of Maliki's "emerging dictatorship" in 2012. AQI/ISI grew in Iraq during this time period out of a complex mix of factors, including Sunni frustration with an exclusionary Maliki government.

Meanwhile, in Syria, violent repression of protests by the Assad regime drove the country into civil war and created the space for Islamist groups to take root. AQI/ISI fighters leveraged their Iraq experience to form Jabhat al-Nusra (JN), whose first attacks occurred in January 2012. The group quickly gained a reputation for being well-organized, fearsome, and skilled. Many fighters, particularly Syrians, came from AQI/ISI and had strong ties with al-Qaeda central.

Is ISIL al-Qaeda?

In April of 2013, Abu Bakr al-Baghdadi, a long-time AQI/ISI fighter who rose through the ISI ranks and replaced Abu Omar al-Baghdadi as leader after his death in 2010, called on all jihadis in Iraq and the "Levant" to unite under his new banner—ISIL—to form an Islamic state. Abu Muhammad al-Joulani, leader of JN in Syria, rejected the merger and re-affirmed his allegiance directly to al-Qaeda leader Ayman al-Zawahiri. Zawahiri attempted to intervene, "giving" Syria to Joulani and Iraq to Baghdadi, but his efforts failed to broker an agreement, leaving a wide schism between ISIL, JN, and al Qaeda. While ISIL maintains similar goals and ideological outlook with al-Qaeda, there is no coordinated command relationship between the two groups; and in Syria there is fierce competition between JN and ISIL for local control. JN remains more formally in al-Qaeda's orbit.

Is ISIL Forming a "State"?

ISIL has engaged in a number of activities in an effort to hold territory and develop a proto-state, imposing taxes and supporting welfare programs and limited public works. They have created a charter outlining new rules in the territory they control, establishing social services, providing religious education, and developing new police and justice systems. There are reports of "jihad taxes" on local businesses in Mosul, with ISIL openly functioning as a "shadow state." And some have argued that they effectively control territory from Raqqa province in Syria through Deir Ezzor and Hasakeh to Anbar (and now Nineveh) province in Iraq. Several contacts in Syria report that the group has established an embassy in Aleppo City, and fighters in the group burned their existing passports and pledged allegiance to the Islamic State in propaganda videos. Their drive to establish border crossing points between Iraq and Syria in southern Hasakeh Province also indicates engagement in core activities of a state.

And while colloquially people know them by their acronym, *Da'esh,* they prefer to be referred as simply *Dawla,* or the state.

Yet for all of these "softer" governance efforts ISIL still largely relies on coercion, especially in Syria, where its brutality is well-documented. For example, ISIL began its control of Raqqa City with a public execution of three Alawites in the town center. It regularly and publicly executes and crucifies Free Syrian Army (FSA) soldiers and various "enemies" to suppress dissent. While ISIL shows growing awareness of the importance of addressing civilian needs in Syria, such as public works projects, this is not their normal *modus operandi.* "They just take from people in Syria," explained one activist from al-Tabqa, who noted that ISIL restricts the flow of basic goods like flour and electricity to punish communities under its control. ISIL has also largely banned cooperation with international relief agencies like the Red Crescent, preventing humanitarian aid from reaching many besieged communities in Syria.

This coercion is in contrast to JN, which has engaged in substantial efforts to provide aid and services to local communities, such asdelivering bread in the southern province of Deraa, repairing roads in Idlib, and providing bus services in Aleppo City. JN has also avoided targeting minority communities and made an effort to minimize damage to civilian areas during military attacks. These efforts indicate an evolution from their AQI predecessors, moving away from nihilistic coercion toward a more Hezbollah-like model that blends military strength and local governance.

It remains to be seen whether ISIL will continue to develop its administrative functions providing services and protecting local civilians—as it claims to be doing in Mosul—or whether ISIL will revert to form in Iraq and govern as it does in Raqqa (and as it once did in Anbar).

Did ISIL Defeat the Iraqi army in Mosul?

We identified a number of institutional and political challenges that left the 2nd Division of the Iraqi Army—which bears primary responsibility for military operations against ISIL in Neneveh province where Mosul is located—vulnerable to the sudden collapse it experienced in early June.Corruption, neglect, and a shortfall of combat-effective resources and personnel crippled the Iraqi military's capability and widened ISIL's range of strategic options in Nineveh.

There is no doubt that ISIL has grown militarily in the past four years, while nurturing alliances of opportunity with other Sunni militant groups in Iraq (alliances that already show signs of fraying). But that was not the sole cause of their recent gains in Mosul and Tikrit. Iraqi Security Forces (ISF) did not collapse overnight: they had been failing for over a year before they finally crumbled on June 10th. In areas such as Fallujah, it took extended guerrilla operations and urban warfare to keep out government forces, but in Mosul, Tikirit, and other recent ISIL offensives, retreat was voluntary and disorganized rather than forced by similarly heavy fighting. In fact, many soldiers reported their positions collapsed without a shot fired. The army left behind weapons, vehicles, uniforms, and no government opposition to ISIL within Mosul itself.

How Corrupt is the Iraqi Army?

In the Iraqi army, leadership at the division level maintains enough sway over logistics and pay to embezzle and extort lower ranks. Many officers see their units as businesses with reliable revenues rather than combat outfits. "You don't earn a [commanding position]: you buy it," a Captain in the Iraqi Army commented. The administrative structure of Iraqi forces aggravates this problem. For example, high-ranking officers are supposed to budget food purchases for their soldiers and deduct money for them out of their salaries. In practice, officers pocket most of this money, and establish revenue quotas for subordinates. Soldiers in Mosul often had to purchase their own food and water from civilian markets and cook themselves, introducing additional duties into already undesirably long working hours. Practices such as selling valuable fuel on the civilian black market and the embezzlement of money meant for food reduce readiness and willingness to fight. "[Corruption] takes more than soldiers' food rations. It takes their dignity and self-respect as well," an Iraqi officer explained. These units are left with a command climate where illicit payments are more important than effective operations or combat performance.

Although many forms of corruption are detrimental to soldiers, some create mutually-beneficial arrangements. Higher-ranking officers often keep absent soldiers on the payroll, offering soldiers the opportunity to leave or never even report for duty in exchange for pocketing a portion of their salaries. Consequently, many estimates of Iraqi force strength include these absent soldiers, dubbed "aliens." Not only do these practices reduce manpower, they also undermine the unit cohesion of soldiers still on the battlefield. In Mosul this was further compounded by ISIL assassinations of soldiers returning from leave. For many, incentives to desert or go AWOL became compelling.

On paper, the 2nd Division appears modern in structure with overwhelming advantage in manpower and firepower. In practice, these units are undermanned, underequipped, undertrained and lack adequate morale for the strain of prolonged urban operations or manoeuvre operations against ISIL.

5

Islamic State of Iraq and the Levant (ISIL) Terror Members

ABDEL-MAJED ABDEL BARY

Abdel-Majed Abdel Bary (born in c.1990) is a British-Egyptian rapper from West London also known as Lyricist Jinn and L Jinny. After circulation of video footage related to the decapitation of the American journalist James Foley, the British intelligence has reportedly centered on three suspects who might be the militant individual in the footage dubbed "Jihadi John", putting a knife to Foley's throat and later on boasting his beheading. The main suspect for being the "Jihadi John" is Abdel Bary himself, with the other two being Abu Hussain Al-Britani, 20, a computer hacker from Birmingham, and Abu Abdullah al-Britani, in his twenties from Portsmouth.

Biography

Abdel-Majed Abdel Bary is the son of Adel Abdel Bari and of Ragaa. His father Adel Mohammed Abdel Magid Abdel Bari (or Bary), was arrested when the youngster Abdel-Majed Abdel Bary was just six. His father was reportedly tortured in Egypt as a suspected radical Islamist.

After release, he moved to the United Kingdom where he applied for political asylum with his wife and family. After a very long process of investigation, with possible returning of Adel Abdel Bary to Egypt, he was extradited eventually by the British authorities to the United States in 2012 for suspected involvement in the 1998 United States embassy bombings in Kenya and Tanzania and for having alleged links and a longtime association with Osama bin Laden and more prominently Ayman al-Zawahiri, current leader of al Qaeda. He is still awaiting trial.

Abdel Bary released a number of recordings about his own predicament as a youth in London. In lyrics for earlier releases online going back to 2012, Bary made apparent references to drug use, violence and life on a council estate and talked about the threat of his family being deported to Egypt. He also appeared in SBTV Warmup Sessions as Lyricist Jinn presenting two live tracks that talked about his experiences. In later songs however, references to cannabis use stopped in his lyrics to be replaced with more radical tirades against people who choose to spend their money clubbing, drinking and on drugs rather than feeding their families. He was also part of a rap group known as The Black Triangle.

Known tracks by him include "Overdose" (the only one uploaded to his YouTube channel LJinnyVEVO), "Flying High", "Dreamer" and "The Beginning". Some of his recordings were reportedly picked up on BBC Radio 1. As late as December 1, 2013, music featuring L. Jinny was still being released including the track "My Words" featuring L Jinny on the album *More True Talk* by Logic & Last Resort.

Abdel-Majed Abdel Bary was radicalised by Muslim groups in England. His father's legal ordeal and his eventual extradition to the States greatly affected Abdel-Majed Abdel Bary and served in radicalising him further. On July 1, 2013, he reportedly announced that he was giving up his musical aspirations for Islam. "I have left everything for the sake of Allah" he said walking out of his family's home in Maida Vale, inGreater London, leaving behind his mother Ragaa and his five siblings. That year, he joined the jihadist opposition forces in Syria for fighting the Syrian regime of President Bashar al-Assad. In March 2014, he had a run-in with rival Free Syrian Army opposition forces claiming in a tweet that he was kidnapped and tortured by them. He eventually joined the even more radical Islamic State of Iraq and the Levant (ISIL / ISIS).

In June 2014, *The Sunday Times* revealed a threat made by Bary on Twitter saying: "The lions are coming for you soon you filthy kuffs (infidels). Beheadings in your own backyard soon."

In early August 2014, he posted a photograph of himself holding a man's severed head allegedly taken in Raqqa, Syria, the stronghold of ISIL and declared capital for the ISIL self-proclaimed Islamic State. The caption read: "Chillin' with my homie or what's left of him." *The Sunday Times* and *Sunday People* listed Bary as a member of a group of at least three British-born ISIS fighters that guarded foreign hostages in Syria, a group they called "The Beatles" being "John", "George" and "Ringo" because of their British accents. According to *The Daily Mail*, the suspected executioner in the Foley video is "John the Beatle". A representative of the Scotland Yard told *Billboard*magazine that the man in the video has not definitely been identified.

ABU BAKR AL-BAGHDADI

Ibrahim ibn Awwad ibn Ibrahim ibn Ali ibn Muhammad al-Badri al-Samarrai, formerly also known as Abu Du'a, most commonly known by the nom de guerre Abu Bakr al-Baghdadi, and in an attempt to claim him as a descendant of Muhammad, more recently as Abu Bakr Al-Baghdadi Al-Husseini Al-Qurashi and now as Amir al-Mu'minin Caliph Ibrahim, has been named the Caliph—head of state and theocratic absolute monarch—of the self-proclaimed Islamic State located in westernIraq and north-eastern Syria. He is the former leader of the Islamic State of Iraq and the Levant(ISIL), alternatively translated as the Islamic State in Iraq and Syria (ISIS).

On 4 October 2011, the US State Department listed al-Baghdadi as a Specially Designated Global Terrorist and announced a reward of up to US$10 million for information leading to his capture or death. Only Ayman al-Zawahiri, chief of the global al-Qaeda organization, merits a larger reward (US$25 million).

Background

Al-Baghdadi is believed to have been born near Samarra, Iraq, in 1971. According to an alleged biography posted on jihadist internet forums in July 2013, he obtained a BA, an MAand a PhD degree in Islamic studies from the Islamic University of Baghdad —since renamed the Iraqi University—in Adhamiya, Baghdad. Reports suggest that he was a cleric at the Imam Ahmad ibn Hanbal Mosque in Samarra at around the time of the US-led invasion of Iraq in 2003.

Militant Activity

After the US invasion of Iraq in 2003, al-Baghdadi helped to found the militant group Jamaat Jaysh Ahl al-Sunnah wa-l-Jamaah (JJASJ), in which he served as head of the group's sharia committee. Al-Baghdadi and his group joined the Mujahideen Shura Council (MSC) in 2006, in which he served as a member of the MSC's sharia committee. Following the renaming of the MSC as the Islamic State of Iraq (ISI) in 2006, al-Baghdadi became the general supervisor of the ISI's sharia committee and a member of the group's senior consultative council.

According to US Department of Defense records, al-Baghdadi was held at Camp Buccaas a "civilian internee" by US Forces-Iraq from February until December 2004, when he was recommended for an "unconditional release" by a Combined Review and Release Board. A number of newspapers, in contrast, have stated that al-Baghdadi was interned from 2005 to 2009. These reports originated in an interview of Army Col Kenneth King, the former commander of Camp Bucca, and are not substantiated by US Department of Defense records.

As Leader of the Islamic State in Iraq

The Islamic State of Iraq (ISI)—also known as Al-Qaeda in Iraq or AQI—was the Iraqi division of the international Islamist militant organization al-Qaeda. Al-Baghdadi was announced as leader of the ISI on 16 May 2010, following the death of his predecessor Abu Omar al-Baghdadi in a raid the month before.

As leader of the ISI, al-Baghdadi was responsible for managing and directing large-scale operations such as the 28 August 2011 attack on the Umm al-Qura mosque in Baghdad which killed prominent Sunni lawmaker Khalid al-Fahdawi. Between March and April 2011, the ISI claimed 23 attacks south of Baghdad, all of which were alleged to have been carried out under al-Baghdadi's command.

Following the US commando raid on 2 May 2011 in Abbottabad, Pakistan, that killed al-Qaeda supreme leader Osama bin Laden, al-Baghdadi released a statement eulogizing bin Laden and threatening violent retaliation for his death. On 5 May 2011, al-Baghdadi claimed responsibility for an attack in Hilla that killed 24 policemen and wounded 72 others.

On 15 August 2011, a wave of ISI suicide attacks beginning in Mosul resulted in 70 deaths. Shortly thereafter, the ISI pledged on its website to carry out 100 attacks across Iraq in retaliation for bin Laden's death. It stated that this campaign would feature various methods of attack, including raids, suicide attacks, roadside bombs and small arms attacks, in all cities and rural areas across the country.

On 22 December 2011, a series of coordinated car bombings and IED attacks struck over a dozen neighborhoods across Baghdad, killing at least 63 people and wounding 180; the assault came just days after the US completed its troop withdrawal from the country.

On 26 December, the ISI released a statement on jihadist internet forums claiming credit for the operation, stating that the targets of the Baghdad attack were "accurately surveyed and explored" and that the "operations were distributed between targeting security headquarters, military patrols and gatherings of the filthy ones of the al-Dajjal Army", referring to the Mahdi Army of Shia warlord Muqtada al-Sadr.

On 2 December 2012, Iraqi officials claimed that they had captured al-Baghdadi in Baghdad following a two-month tracking operation. Officials claimed that they had also seized a list containing the names and locations of other al-Qaeda operatives. However, this claim was rejected by the ISI. In an interview with Al Jazeera on 7 December 2012, Iraq's Acting Interior Minister said that the arrested man was not al-Baghdadi, but rather a section commander in charge of an area stretching from the northern outskirts of Baghdad to Taji.

As Leader of the Islamic State of Iraq and the Levant

Al-Baghdadi remained leader of the ISI until its formal expansion into Syria in 2013, when in a statement on 8 April 2013, he announced the formation of the Islamic State of Iraq and the Levant (ISIL)—alternatively translated from the Arabic as the Islamic State in Iraq and Syria(ISIS). As the leader of ISIS, al-Baghdadi took charge of running all ISIS activity in Iraq and Syria.

When announcing the formation of ISIS, al-Baghdadi stated that the Syrian Civil War jihadist faction, Jabhat al-Nusra—also known as al-Nusra Front—had been an extension of the ISI in Syria and was now to be merged with ISIS.

The leader of Jabhat al-Nusra, Abu Mohammad al-Jawlani, disputed this merging of the two groups and appealed to al-Qaeda emir Ayman al-Zawahiri, who issued a statement that ISIS should be abolished and that al-Baghdadi should confine his group's activities to Iraq. Al-Baghdadi, however, dismissed al-Zawahiri's ruling and took control of a reported 80% of Jabhat al-Nusra's foreign fighters. In January 2014, ISIS expelled Jabhat al-Nusra from the Syrian city of Raqqa, and in the same month clashes between the two in Syria's Deir ez-Zor Governorate killed hundreds of fighters and displaced tens of thousands of civilians. In February 2014, al-Qaeda disavowed any relations with ISIS.

According to several Western sources, al-Baghdadi and ISIS have received private financing from citizens in Saudi Arabia and Qatar and enlisted fighters through recruitment drives in Saudi Arabia in particular.

As Caliph of the Islamic State

On 29 June 2014, ISIS announced the establishment of a caliphate, al-Baghdadi was named its caliph, to be known as Caliph Ibrahim, and the Islamic State of Iraq and the Levant was renamed the Islamic State (IS). There has been much debate across the Muslim world about the legitimacy of these moves.

The declaration of a caliphate has been heavily criticized by Middle Eastern governments and other jihadist groups, and by Sunni Muslim theologians and historians. Yusuf al-Qaradawi, a prominent scholar living in Qatar stated: "[The] declaration issued by the Islamic State is void under sharia and has dangerous consequences for the Sunnis in Iraq and for the revolt in Syria", adding that the title of caliph can "only be given by the entire Muslim nation", not by a single group.

In an audio-taped message, al-Baghdadi announced that ISIS would march on Rome in its quest to establish an Islamic State from the Middle East across Europe, saying that he would conquer both Rome and Spain in this endeavor. He also urged Muslims across the world to emigrate to the new Islamic State.

On 5 July 2014, a video was released apparently showing al-Baghdadi making a speech at the Great Mosque of al-Nuri in Mosul, northernIraq. A representative of the Iraqi government denied that the video was of al-Baghdadi, calling it a "farce". However, both the BBC and the Associated Press quoted unnamed Iraqi officials as saying that the man in the video was believed to be al-Baghdadi. In the video, al-Baghdadi declared himself the world leader of Muslims and called on Muslims everywhere to support him.

ABU MOHAMMAD AL-ADNANI

Shaykh Abu Mohammad al-Adnani al-Shami, whose original name is likely Taha Subhi Falaha, the officialspokesman and a chief leader of the Islamic state, was born in 1977 in the town of Binnish of the Idlib Governorate, in western Syria. He was reportedly one of the first foreign fighters to oppose Coalition forces in Iraq.

On 18 August 2014, the US State Department listed al-Adnani as a Specially Designated Global Terrorist.

ABU OMAR AL-SHISHANI

Tarkhan Batirashvili (born 1986), more commonly known by his nom de guerre Abu Omar al-Shishani or Omar al-Shishani, is an ethnic Georgian, a Kist (Chechens from Georgia) from his mother's side, and a leader of the Islamic State of Iraq and the Levant in Syria. Batirashvili was the leader of the rebel group *Katibat al-Muhajireen* (Emigrants Brigade), also known as theMuhajireen Brigade, and its successor, Jaish al-Muhajireen wal-Ansar (Army of Emigrants and Supporters).

Batirashvili was named commander of the northern sector of Syria by the Islamic State of Iraq and the Levant (ISIS) in the summer of 2013. Units under his command have participated in major assaults on Syrian military bases in and around Aleppo, including the capture of Menagh Airbase in August 2013. He is considered "one of the most influential military leaders of the Syrian opposition forces". It has been speculated that he may have become the military chief for ISIS following the death of Abu Abdul-Rahman al-Bilawi al-Anbari in Mosul in June 2014.

Early Life

Batirashvili was born in 1986 into an ethnic Georgian-Kist family. His father belongs to the Georgian gvari Batirashvili and his mother belonged to the Melkhi clan. His father, Timur Batirashvilli, is an ethnic Georgian Orthodox Christian and his mother was a Muslim. Their village of Birkiani is located in Georgia's Pankisi Gorge, which was a major transit point for rebels participating in the Second Chechen War, and according to his father, a young Batirashvili secretly helped Chechen militants into Russia and sometimes joined them on missions against Russian-backed troops.

Military Service

Following high school, Batirashvili joined the Georgian Army and distinguished himself as master of various weaponry and maps, according to his former commander Malkhaz Topuria, who recruited him into a special reconnaissance group. He rose to the rank of sergeant in a newly formed intelligence unit, and during the 2008 Russia-Georgia War he served near the front line, spying on Russian tank columns and relaying their coordinates to Georgian artillery units.

Batirashvili was never decorated for his military service, and in 2010 he was diagnosed with tuberculosis. After being hospitalized for several months, he was released and deemed unfit for the military and discharged. Upon returning home, he was unable to secure work in the local police force and became "very disillusioned", according to his father.

Militant Activity

According to the Georgian Defense Ministry, Batirashvili was arrested in September 2010 for illegally harboring weapons and was sentenced to three years in prison. He was allegedly released after serving about 16 months in early 2012 and immediately left the country. According to an interview on a jihadist website, Batirashvili said that prison transformed him; "I promised God that if I come out of prison alive, I'll go fight jihad for the sake of God", he said.

Batirashvili reportedly told his father that he was leaving for Istanbul, where members of the Chechen diaspora were ready to recruit him to lead fighters inside war-ravaged Syria; an older brother had already gone to Syria some months before. In an interview, Batirashvili said that he had considered going to Yemen and briefly lived in Egypt before ultimately arriving in Syria in March 2012.

His first command was the Muhajireen Brigade, an Islamist jihadist group made up of foreign fighters that was formed in the summer of 2012. His unit became involved in the Battle of Aleppo, and in October 2012 they assisted the Al-Nusra Front in a raid on an air defense and Scud missile base in Aleppo.

In December 2012, they fought alongside Al-Nusra Front during the overrunning of the Sheikh Suleiman Army base in Western Aleppo. In February 2013, together with the Tawhid Brigades and Al-Nusra Front, they stormed the base of the Syrian military's 80th Regiment near the main airport in Aleppo.

In March 2013, the Kavkaz Center reported that the Muhajireen Brigade had merged with two Syrianjihadist groups called Jaish Muhammad and Kataeb Khattab to form a new group called Jaish Muhajireen wal-Ansar, or Army of Emigrants and Helpers. The group's leadership structure consists of a military leadership, a sharia committee, a shura council and a media arm, Liwa al-Mujahideen al-Ilami. The latter is the same name as a media group established by foreign mujahideen fighting in the Bosnian war.

The group played a key role in the August 2013 capture of Menagh Air Base, which culminated in a Vehicle Borne Improvised Explosive Device (VBIED) driven by two of their members killing and wounding many of the last remaining Syrian Armed Forces defenders. A branch of the Muhajireen Brigade was involved in the 2013 Latakia offensive.

In August 2013, Batirashvili released a statement announcing the expulsion of one of his commanders, Emir Seyfullah, and 27 of his men from the group. Batirashvili accused the men of embezzlement and stirring up the animosity of local Syrians against the foreign fighters by indulging in takfir—excommunication—against other Muslims. However, Seyfullah denied these allegations in a statement and claimed that it was because he had refused to join the Islamic State of Iraq and the Levant with Batirashvili.

In late 2013, Batirashvili was replaced as leader of Jaish al-Muhajireen wala-Ansar by another Chechen commander known as Salahuddin, as most of the Chechen members of the group did not support Batirashvili's oath of allegiance to the Islamic State of Iraq and the Levant in November due to their preexisting oath to Dokka Umarov, leader of the Caucasus Emirate.

For a time, Batirashvili lived with his family in a large villa owned by a businessman in the town of Huraytan just northwest of Aleppo.

ABU WAHEEB

Shaker Wahib al-Fahdawi, known as *Abu Waheeb* ("Father of the Generous") is a leader of Islamic State in Iraq and the Levant forces in Anbar, Iraq.

Fahdawi was born in 1986. In 2006, whilst studying computer science at the University of Anbar, he was arrested by US forces on charges of belonging to Al-Qaeda in Iraq. Following Fahdawi's arrest he was detained by US forces at the Camp Bucca detention facility in southern Iraq until 2009, when he was sentenced to death and moved to Tikrit Central Prison in Saladin Province.

Fahdawi was one of 110 detainees who managed to escape the prison in 2012, following a riot and an attack on the prison by forces from the Islamic State of Iraq.

Following his escape he became an ISI field commander in Anbar province, having been trained and prepared during his incarceration. The two prisons he had been housed at had previously held a large number of ISI leaders. Since his escape he has been active in anti-government operations, with his appearances becoming more brazen. Iraqi officials have blamed him for a litany of terror-related offences. Anbar Security Officials have put a $50,000 bounty out for him.

JIHADI JOHN

Jihadi John is the nickname given by news media to an unidentified member of theIslamic State of Iraq and the Levant (ISIS) who appears in a video of August 19, 2014 to be beheading the US photojournalist James Foley.

Jihadi John got his nickname from a group of released hostages who claim he is the leader of a terrorist cell called "The Beatles" and handles relations with families of foreign hostages. The nickname is based on the pop group The Beatles, with other members of the cell known as "George" and "Ringo".

Execution of James Foley

In a video uploaded to YouTube on August 19, 2014, Foley read a prepared statement criticizing America, the recent airstrikes in Iraq and his brother who serves in the Air Force. Jihadi John, wearing a mask, also read a prepared statement in which he criticized America andPresident Obama. The masked man then beheaded James Foley, with the act taking place off camera. The FBI and United States National Security Council confirmed that the video, which included footage of Mr Foley's beheaded corpse, is genuine.

The video was produced and distributed by Al Hayat Media Center, a media outlet of IS that is under the authority of the IS's official propaganda arm, the Al-Itisam Establishment for Media Production, that targets specifically Western and non-Arabic speaking audiences. Jihadi John is currently the subject of a manhunt by the FBI, MI5 and Scotland Yard.

Analysis of the Video

Officially the FBI and United States National Security Council confirmed that the video, which ended with footage of Foley's beheaded corpse, is genuine.

Unofficially, an unnamed forensics expert commissioned by *The Times* to look at the video said "I think it has been staged. My feeling is that the execution may have happened after the camera was stopped." *The Times* concluded that "No one is questioning that the photojournalist was beheaded, but camera trickery and slick post-production techniques appear to have been used." Two unnamed video specialists in the *International Business Times of Australia* claimed that portions of the video appeared to be staged and edited. Dr. James Alvarez, a British-American hostage negotiator, also claimed the video was "expertly staged".

British analyst Eliot Higgins (Brown Moses) published photographic and video forensic evidence suggesting that the video was taken at a spot in the hills south of the Syrian city of Raqqa.

Execution of a Syrian Soldier

In a video posted on Instagram in May 2014, a man who investigators believe may be Jihadi John is seen in a video killing a Syrian soldier. It shows a soldier loyal to President Bashar al-Assad crouching in a field in Syria, then being shot in the back of the head by a man armed with a pistol.

Other Hostages

Apart from Foley, Jihadi John claims that he has over 20 hostages remaining, including another American journalist named Steven Joel Sotloff, who is seen at the end of Foley's beheading video.

Identification and Manhunt

Several facts about Jihadi John can be ascertained from the Foley video. He spoke with a "Multicultural London English" accent, appears to be left handed and appears to have a skin tone consistent with African or South Asian descent. Other factors that could lead to his identification are his height, general physique, the pattern of veins on the back of his hand, his voice and clothes. A team of analysts might use the topography of the landscape in the video in an attempt to identify the location.

On 24 August 2014, the British Ambassador to Washington, Sir Peter Westmacott, said that Britain was very close to identifying Jihadi John using sophisticated voice recognition technology but when pressed, refused to disclose any more details

Possible Identity

On August 24, 2014, it was reported that MI5 and MI6 were investigating three men who left the U.K. for Syria to fight with the Islamic State of Iraq and the Levant. The key suspect is Abdel-Majed Abdel Bary, a hip hop artist from London, and the son of Egyptian militant Adel Abdel Bari. Other suspects include Abu Hussain Al-Britani, a computer hacker from Birmingham; and Abu Abdullah al-Britani from Portsmouth.

DOUGLAS MCCAIN

Douglas McAuthur McCain (January 29, 1981 – August 23/24, 2014) was a US-born jihadist who was killed in Syria in late August 2014 fighting for the Islamic State of Iraq and the Levant in an encounter with the Syrian Free Army. Originally from San Diego, California, McCain, a graduate fromRobbinsdale Cooper High School in New Hope, Minnesota, converted to Islam in 2004, and traveled to Syria by way of Turkey in early 2014. He was the first known American to be killed while fighting for the Islamic State. At the time of McCain's death, there were reportedly "dozens" more Americans fighting in Syria for Islamic militant groups. The first American killed fighting in the Syrian Civil War was Moner Mohammad Abu-Salha in May 2014. McCain attended the same high school as did Troy Kastigar, another American who died as a jihadist, in 2009 in Somalia. The two may have been roommates.

Biography

McCain was born in San Diego, California, then moved to Minnesota. He attended Robbinsdale Cooper High School from

1997-99, before transferring to nearby Robbinsdale Armstrong High School; he never graduated. Robbinsdale Cooper was also the school Kastigar had attended. McCain may have lived in Kastigar's house for a while, in 2000 and 2001. He loved basketball and was a fan of the Chicago Bulls. McCain racked up a criminal record with minor charges including traffic violations, disorderly conduct, and giving false names to police offers; by 2004 he had converted to Islam (according to a Tweet ten years later in which he said it was "the best thing that ever happen[ed]" to him). He traveled to Europe, and by 2013 was back in San Diego where he worked in a mosque (other sources say he worked in Somali restaurant, and "frequented" a mosque).

According to a former classmate he was eager to talk about Islam and his conversion, but remained respectful of others' beliefs and was not radical. He was active on social media, with the handle "Duale Khalid" on Twitter and "Duale ThaslaveofAllah" on Facebook.

McCain was killed in fights with the Free Syrian Army in the weekend of August 23/24, 2014, and was found with $800 in cash on his body and a US passport.

ABU SULEIMAN AL-NASER

Abu Suleiman al-Naser is the "war minister" of the Islamic State of Iraq (ISI). Little is known about Abu Suleiman. He succeeded Abu Ayyub al-Masri, the leader of al-Qaeda in Iraq who was killed along with ISI leader Abu Omar al-Baghdadi in a joint operation by US and Iraqi forces in Tikrit in April 2010, as the Minister of War for the Islamic State of Iraq. The new war minister signed with the name *Al-Nasser Lideen Allah Abu Suleiman*, a nom de guerre that translates "Defender of God's Religion, Father of Suleiman". His real name is Neaman Salman Mansour al Zaidi. Iraqi security forces claimed to have killed Suleiman in February 2011 in the town of Hît, west of Baghdad. However, the ISI denied his death a month later.

6

Persecution of Yazidis by the Islamic State

The persecution of Yazidis by the Islamic State refers to the genocidal persecution of the Yazidi people of Iraq, leading to their exile, abduction of their women and massacres, during what has been called a "forced conversion campaign" being carried out in Northern Iraq by the militant organization Islamic State.

The IS's persecution of the Yazidi has gained international attention, with the United States taking military action against IS militants with airstrikes and ground troops. Additionally, the US, UK and France have made emergency airdrops to the besieged Yazidi and provided weapons to the Kurdish Peshmerga defending them. The IS's actions against the Yazidi population have resulted in tens of thousands of refugees, hundreds murdered and hundreds kidnapped.

Background

The Yazidis are the latest minority group that the ISIL has targeted in its campaign of religious persecution and the killing of those different from themselves and those unwilling to convert to Islam. The other minorities who face danger from the ISIL are the Shabaks, whose faith is similar to that of the Yazidis, the Turkmens and the Assyrians.

The Yazidi are monotheists who believe in a benevolent peacock angel (Melek Taus) and whose ancient gnostic faith has elements of Zoroastrianism, Christianity and Islam. The Islamic State of Iraq and the Levant and other extremists tend to view the peacock angel as the malevolent archangel Lucifer or Satan and label the Yazidi as 'devil' worshippers.

Under Islamic law as observed by the ISIL, Yazidis are officially given the choice to convert to Sunni Islam or die. They are not eligible for the tax taken from "People of the Book" by the ISIL that would allow them to continue observing their religion. These persecutions and murders are motivated by the ISIL's interpretation of verse 9:5 of the Koran.

The Yazidi have been targeted by Sunnis before. Two large-scale massacres were conducted by Ottoman forces in the name of Islam.

In 1640, 40,000 Ottoman soldiers attacked Yazidi communities around Mount Sinjar, killing 3,060 Yazidis during battle, then raiding and setting fire to 300 Yazidi villages and murdering 1,000–to 2,000 Yazidis who had taken refuge in caves around the town of Sinjar; in 1892, Sultan Abdulhamid II ordered a campaign of mass conscription or murder of Yazidis as part of his campaign to islamize the Ottoman empire, which also targeted Armenians and other Christians. In 2007, two Yazidi communities were hit by a total of four vehicle bombs carrying two tons of explosives, leaving 796 dead and 1,562 injured.

Violence Outbreak

Many Yazidis have reported summary executions by IS militants, leading to around 50,000–60,000 Yazidis from Sinjar escaping from the IS to the nearby Sinjar mountain. They were besieged by the IS on Mount Sinjar, facing starvation and dehydration. On 3 August 2014, IS militants attacked and took over Sinjar, a Kurdish-controlled town that was home to Yazidis. On 4 August 2014, Prince Tahseen Said, Emir of the Yazidi, issued a plea to world leaders calling for assistance on behalf of the Yazidi facing attack from the Islamic State.

SINJAR MASSACRE

The Sinjar massacre was conducted by Islamic State (shortened IS, ISIL or ISIS) as part of the August 2014 offensive. Sinjar was one of many towns captured during the Islamic State's offensive in early August 2014. Zumar was alsotaken over by ISIS, as well as the Mosul Dam. Kurds appealed to the Government of Iraq and the United States for air support to assist their cause. Kurdish army officials Peshmerga also said to a newspaper in an interview that air strikes are needed badly to stop a possible ISIS invasion into Iraqi Kurdistan.

On 7 August, the U.S. President, Barack Obama, stated that the U.S. would use air power to assist trapped civilians threatened with acts of genocide and attack ISIS forces. Obama stated that his decision was made because U.S. "leadership is necessary to underwrite the global security and prosperity", "to protect our [American] people," to "support our allies," to "lead coalitions of countries to uphold international norms," "to prevent a potential act of genocide," and to "strive to stay true to the fundamental values—the desire to live with basic freedom and dignity."

Background

Sinjar was a predominantly-Yazidi before the ISIS takeover, and the invasion forced most to leave their homes. ISIS declared a Caliphate in June 2014 in areas of Syria and Iraq and have since gained more areas in Iraq.

ISIS take Over

On the morning of 3 August, ISIS forces advanced into and captured Sinjar. According to the United Nations, thousands of refugees were expelled from the city and lacked basic amenities. In parallel, the humanitarian disaster drew a harsh response by the Kurdish military Peshmerga and ISIS faced the first great resistance after its offensive in Iraq in June 2014. According to some reports as many as 500 Yazidis were massacred in the ISIS attack and its aftermath, and dozens more died of hunger, while fleeing the ISIS advance.

Tahseen Said, Emir of the Yazidis, issued a plee on 4 August 2014 to world leaders, concerning the plight of the people being attacked by the Islamic State. The Yazidis were besieged by IS on Mount Sinjar, facing starvation and dehydration.

U.S. Airstrikes and Humanitarian Aid

On 8 August, US F/A-18 fighters bombed ISIS artillery units. Four U.S. fighters later bombed an Islamic State military convoy. Another round of U.S. airstrikes in the afternoon struck 8 Islamic State targets near Erbil. Armed drones as well as fixed wing aircraft were used in the U.S. attacks. U.S. and U.K. planes dropped food and water for Yazidis stranded on the Sinjar Mountains and surrounded by IS forces firing on them, while France pledged aid to refugees.

On 12 August, an Iraqi military helicopter, piloted by Maj. Gen. Majid Ahmed Saadi, crashed in the mountains while delivering aid and rescuing stranded Yazidi refugees. The helicopter was also carrying Yazidi lawmakers and foreign journalists. The general was the only fatality in the crash, while almost all of the passengers were injured.

On 14 August, U.S air-strikes and Kurdish fighters of the People's Protection Units from Syria, together with their PKK allies from Turkey, had broken the ISIS siege of Mount Sinjar, allowing thousands of refugees to escape.

Massacres, Human Trafficking and Forced Exile

On 5 August 2014, Al Jazeera reported that an Islamic State offensive in the Sinjar area of northern Iraq had forced 30,000–50,000 Yazidisto flee into the mountains fearing they would be killed by the IS. They had been threatened with death if they refused conversion to Islam. A UN representative said that "a humanitarian tragedy is unfolding in Sinjar". The next day IS kidnapped 400 Yazidi women in Sinjar to sell them as sex slaves. On 10 August 2014, IS militants buried alive an undefined number of Yazidi women and children in an attack that killed 500 people, in what has been described as ongoing genocide in northern Iraq.

According to a statement by the Iraqi government on 10 August 2014, hundreds of women were taken as slaves and 500 Yazidis murdered by the IS, some of them being buried alive. Those who escaped across the Tigris River into Kurdish-controlled areas of Syria on 10 August gave accounts of how they had seen individuals also attempting to flee who later died.

A further atrocity was reported against the Yazidi village of Kojo, south of Sinjar, where after the whole population received the customary jihadist ultimatum to convert or be killed, over 80 men were killed and over 100 women abducted on 15 August. A witness recounted that like elsewhere the villagers were first converted under duress, but when the village elder refused to convert all men were taken in trucks under the pretext of being led to Sinjar, and gunned down by surprise along the way.

In several villages, local Sunnis were reported to have sided with IS, betraying Yazidis for slaughter once IS arrived, and even possibly colluding in advance with IS to lie to Yazidis to lure them into staying put until the jihadis invaded; although there was also one report of Sunnis helping Yazidis escape.

International Responses

Turkish Aid

Hundreds and possibly thousands of Yazidis have taken refuge in neighboring Turkey, where they are being sheltered in refugee camps in the city of Silopi. The Turkish Disaster Relief Agency (AFAD) has begun preparations to set up camps for receiving 6,000 refugees from Iraq. The number of Yazidi refugees in Turkey has reached 14 thousand by August 30.

Turkey has also airdropped humanitarian aid to Yazidi refugees within Iraq.

United States' Support

On 7 August 2014, a high-level meeting was held at the White House to discuss the situation. During the meeting, talks included plans for targeted airstrikes on IS militants and emergency air relief for the Yazidis. On 8 August 2014, the US asserted that the systematic destruction of the Yazidi people by the Islamic State is genocide. The US military launched indefinite airstrikes targeting Islamic State fighters, equipment and installations, with humanitarian aid support from the UK and France, in order to protect civilians in northern Iraq. On 9 August 2014, at approximately 11:20 a.m. ET, the United States began targeted airstrikes on IS militants, when two IS armored personnel carriers (APCs) firing on Yazidis were destroyed. Three additional airstrikes occurred when additional IS APCs entered the area, and ISIS fighters were targeted near the town ofMakhmur, where the group was launching attacks on the outskirts of Irbil. Fighter jets and military drones carried out the airstrikes after President Barack Obama authorized targeted attacks to protect Americans and Iraqi minorities. President Obama also gave an assurance that no troops would be deployed for combat. Along with the airstrikes, the US airdropped 3,804 gallons of water and 16,128 MREs. Following these actions, the United Kingdom and France stated that they also would begin airdrops.

On 10 August 2014, at approximately 2:15 a.m. ET, the US carried out five additional airstrikes on armed vehicles and a mortar position, enabling 20,000–30,000 Yazidi Iraqis to flee into Syria and later be rescued by Kurdish forces. The Kurdish forces then provided shelter for the Yazidis in Dohuk.

On 13 August 2014, fewer than 20 United States Special Forces troops stationed in Irbil along with British Special Air Service troops visited the area near Mount Sinjar to gather intelligence and plan the evacuation of approximately 30,000 Yazidis still trapped on Mount Sinjar.

One hundred and twenty-nine additional US military personnel were deployed to Irbil to assess and provide a report to President Obama. The United States Central Command also reported that a seventh airdrop was conducted and that to date, 114,000 meals and more than 35,000 gallons of water had been airdropped to the displaced Yazidis in the area.

In a statement on 14 August 2014, The Pentagon said that the 20 US personnel who had visited the previous day had concluded that a rescue operation was probably unnecessary since there was less danger from exposure or dehydration and the Yazidis were no longer believed to be at risk of attack from the Islamic State.

Estimates also stated that 4,000 to 5,000 people remained on the mountain, with nearly half of which being Yazidi herders who lived there before the siege. However, Kurdish officials and Yazidi refugees stated that thousands of young, elderly and disabled individuals on the mountain were still vulnerable, with the governor of Kurdistan's Dahuk province, Farhad Atruchi, saying that the assessment was "not correct" and that although people were suffering, "the international community is not moving".

2007 YAZIDI COMMUNITIES BOMBINGS

The 2007 Yazidi communities bombings occurred at around 7:20 pm local time on August 14, 2007, when four co-ordinated suicide bomb attacks detonated in the Yazidi towns ofKahtaniya and Jazeera (Siba Sheikh Khidir), near Mosul.

Iraqi Red Crescent's estimates say the bombs killed 796 and wounded 1,562 people, making this the Iraq War's most deadly car bomb attack during the period of major American combat operations. It was also the second deadliest act of terrorism in history, following only behind the September 11 attacks in the United States.

Tensions and Background

There had been tensions in the area in recent months, particularly between Yazidis and SunniMuslims (Muslims including Arabs and Kurds). Prior to the attack, some Yazidis living in the area received threatening letters calling them "infidels". Leaflets were also distributed denouncing Yazidis as "anti-Islamic" and warning them that an attack was imminent.

The attack might be connected to an incident wherein Du'a Khalil Aswad, a Yaziditeenage woman, was stoned to death. Aswad was believed to have wanted to convert in order to marry a Sunni. Two weeks later, after a video of the stoning appeared on the Internet, Sunni gunmen stopped minibuses filled with Yazidis; 23 Yazidi men were forced from a bus and shot dead.

The Sinjâr area which has a mixed population of Kurds, Turkmen and Arabs was scheduled to vote in a plebiscite on accession to theKurdish region in December 2007. This caused hostility among the neighbouring Arab communities. A force of 600 Kurdish Peshmerga was subsequently deployed in the area, and ditches were dug around Yazidi villages to prevent further attacks.

Details

The blasts targeted a religious minority, the Yazidi. The co-ordinated bombings involved a fuel tanker and three cars. An Iraqi interior ministry spokesman said that two tons of explosives were used in the blasts, which crumbled buildings, trapping entire families beneath mud bricks and other wreckage as entire neighborhoods were flattened. Rescuers dug underneath the destroyed buildings by hand to search for remaining survivors.

"Hospitals here are running out of medicine. The pharmacies are empty. We need food, medicine and water otherwise there will be an even greater catastrophe," said Abdul-Rahim al-Shimari, mayor of the Baaj district, which includes the devastated villages.

Responsibility

The attacks carry Al-Qaeda's signature of multiple simultaneous attacks. No group claimed responsibility for the attack. "We're looking atAl-Qaeda as the prime suspect," said Lieutenant-Colonel Christopher Garver, a United States military spokesman. The group is reported to have distributed leaflets denouncing Yazidis as "anti-Islamic". Others, including Iraq's President, Jalal Talabani, blamed the bombings on "Iraqi Sunni Muslim Arab insurgents" seeking to undercut Premier Maliki's conclave to end political deadlock among the country's leaders.

On September 3, 2007, the U.S. military reportedly killed the mastermind of the bombings, Abu Mohammed al-Afri.

PERSECUTION OF ASSYRIANS BY THE ISLAMIC STATE

Persecution of Assyrians by the Islamic State refers to the persecution of theAssyrian people (otherwise known as Chaldean or Syriac) within Iraq and Syria by the jihadistorganization Islamic State of Iraq and the Levant (ISIS) following its takeover of parts of Northern Iraq in mid 2014.

Background

The mass flight and expulsion of ethnic Assyrians from Iraq is a process which initiated from the beginning of Iraq War in 2003 and continues to this day..

Leaders of Iraq's Assyrian community estimate that over two-thirds of the Iraqi Assyrian population may have fled the country or been internally displaced since the U.S.-led invasion in 2003 until 2011.

Reports suggest that whole neighborhoods of Assyrians have cleared out in the cities of Baghdad and Al-Basrah, and that both Sunni and Shiite insurgent groups and militias have threatened Assyrian Christians.

Following the campaign of the Islamic State of Iraq and the Levant in northern Iraq in August 2014, one quarter of the remaining Iraqi Assyrian Christians fled the Jihadists, finding refuge in Turkey and Iraqi Kurdistan.

Timeline

Fall of Mosul

After the fall of Mosul, ISIS demanded Assyrian Christians in the city to convert to Islam, pay tribute, or face execution, by July 19, 2014. This resulted in a complete Assyrian Christian exodus from Mosul, marking the end of 1600 years of continuous Christian presence. ISIS had also been seen marking Christian homes with the letter *nûn* for *Nassarah* ("Christian").

Mar Behnam Monstery

The Mar Behnam Monastery was seized by ISIS, and its monks were expelled.

Fall of Qaraqosh

By August 7, ISIS captured the primarily Assyrian towns of Qaraqosh, Tel Keppe, Bartella, and Karamlish, prompting the residents to flee.

Reactions

On 2 and 3 August 2014, thousands of Assyrians/Chaldeans/Syriacs of the diaspora protested the persecution of their fellow Assyrians within Iraq and Syria, demanding a United Nations-led creation of a safe haven for minorities in the Nineveh Plains.

ISLAMIC ARMY IN IRAQ

The Islamic Army in Iraq (IAI) is one of a number of underground Islamist militant (or *mujahideen*) organizations formed in Iraq following the 2003 invasion of Iraq by United States and coalition military forces, and the subsequent collapse of the Baathist government headed by Saddam Hussein.

Although it carries an Islamic title, the group combines Islamism with Iraqi nationalism, and has been labelled as "resistance" by Iraq's Sunni Vice-President Tariq al-Hashemidespite regular attacks against Iraqi soldiers and policemen, as well as Shi'ite militias such as the Mahdi Army and the Badr Organization.

Following the Withdrawal of US Forces from Iraq in late 2011, the IAI demobilized and turned towards political activism, setting up the Sunni Popular Movement. The groups turn away from armed opposititon towards activism was criticised by other militant groups, including groups that the IAI had previously allied with such as Jaysh al-Mujihadeen

Since the beginning of 2014 however the group has been active in the ongoing anti-government violence in Anbar and Northern Iraq. The group is primarily active in Diyala and Saladin provinces.

Roots and ideology

The precise details about the emergence of the IAI are unclear, although it is generally assumed that the group was established in the summer of 2003 to fight coalition forces.

When the IAI first formed, it used kidnapping as a means of pursuing its goals. The group also threatened to target the January 2005 elections, although it didn't carry out any such attack. Unlike most resistance movement organizations today, the IAI does not have Salafisttendencies, its primary focus and goal being the expulsion of foreign troops from Iraq. A November 2004 *Washington Post* interview with the group's leader, Ishmael Jubouri, stated that the IAI was predominantly composed of Iraqis (Sunnis, Shiites, Kurds, and Arabs) trying to force foreign troops out of Iraq. The Terrorism Monitor put out by The Jamestown Foundation confirms some of what Jubouri was claiming. In a March 2005 article, it states the group is composed primarily of Sunnis with a much smaller, but still present, Shiite congregation and, in general, is "[an] inclusive Islamic organization with Iraqi nationalist tendencies."

In a November 2006 *al-Jazeera* interview, spokesman Ibrahim al-Shamary expanded on who the IAI considers foreign troops, *"There are two occupations in Iraq. Iran on one side through the militias which they control and through direct involvement with the national guard and the intelligence services, that causes the killing and destruction of the Sunnis... And then there is the American occupation which destroys the Iraqi people."*

The group has released several joint statements with other groups such as Islamic Resistance Movement and the Islamic Front for the Iraqi Resistance, which are known to be of an ikhwan background. In one of these joint statements, six groups (including the IAI) called for Iraqis to participate in the referendum on the October 2005 constitution by voting against it. (This was in conspicuous contrast to al-Qaeda in Iraq, which said that simply participating in voting is a compromise of the fundamentals of Islam, even if one were to vote against it.)

When rumours spread in Iraq of the alleged demolition of the al-Aqsa Mosque, in April 2005, the IAI announced the formation of the "al-Aqsa Support Division." This group was to support the Palestinians in their armed struggle against Israel. The current status of the al-Aqsa Support Division is unknown, leading people to believe that the statement was merely rhetoric.

Foreign Hostages

The group was responsible for the abduction of the following persons who were released unharmed:

- Fereidoun Jahani, Iranian Consul.
- Georges Malbrunot (41) and Christian Chesnot (37), French journalists.
- Marwan Ibrahim al-Kassar and Mohammed Jawdat Hussein, Lebanese electrical workers.
- Angelo Dela Cruz, Filipino truck driver.

- Rosidah Anom and Rafikan Binti Amin, female Indonesian nationals.

The IAI is believed responsible for the execution of the following foreigners:

- Enzo Baldoni, Italian journalist killed on or about August 26, 2004.
- Raja Azad (49), engineer, and Sajad Naeem (29), his driver, Pakistani nationals working in Iraq for a Kuwaiti-based firm killed on or about July 28, 2004.
- Dalibor Lazarevski, Dragan Markovic, and Zoran Naskovski, nationals of Republic of Macedonia, working for United Arab Emirates-basedSoufan Engineering on contracts and subcontracts for the U.S. military and its private contractors. The three were seized in August 2004 and the Macedonian government confirmed their execution by October 21, 2004; receipt of videos depicting two beheadings were announced, but not broadcast, on al-Jazeera TV on October 17, 2004.
- Ronald Schulz, American contract electrician, killed around December 8, 2005.

Other Activities

The Islamic Army in Iraq claimed responsibility for the 1 September 2004, assassination attempt against Iraqi politician Ahmed Chalabi, leader of the Iraqi National Congress, in which two of his bodyguards were killed, two were wounded and two went missing (the IAI admitted capturing one of Chalabi's bodyguards and executing the other), and Chalabi escaped unharmed.

On 22 April 2005, the IAI released a video of their members killing a Bulgarian civilian contractor, who survived after the downing of his helicopter. He was helped to his feet and then shot with 27 rounds of ammunition. The group also claims to have shot down a commercialairliner in Iraq, although officials maintain the accident was caused by fog. The crash killed 34 people.

In 2006, videos were released of their snipers killing coalition forces. The *nom de guerre* of the IAI sniper(s) is "Juba". These sniper videos were distributed for free to Iraqi citizens on CDs as part of a propaganda, recruiting campaign and as a means of waging psychological warfare on coalition forces. Islamic Army videos of attacks on US-led coalition forces are aired on the al-Zawraa TV channel, which is banned in Iraq.

War with al-Qaeda in Iraq

In early 2007, the Islamic Army engaged in an armed conflict against al-Qaeda in Iraq. In June, this ended in a ceasefire between the two rival groups. The IAI was quoted saying *"The most important thing is that it's our common duty to fight the Americans;"* nevertheless, the groups never adopted al-Qaeda's philosophy and refused to sign on to the al-Qaeda-led Islamic State of Iraq.

According to Iraqi sources, fighters from the Islamic Army battled al-Qaeda gunmen around Samarra at least twice in October and November 2007, a possible indication that the cease-fire brokered earlier this year had collapsed (however, coalition officials later issued a statement claiming that Iraqi policemen and coalition troops, not Islamic Army fighters, had carried out the latter operation). Furthermore, although the Islamic Army denied that it had joined forces with the U.S. military, several news outlets reported that many Islamic Army commanders in and around Baghdad were now working together with the U.S.-led coalition to counter al-Qaeda in Iraq militants and Shia militias.

Bibliography

Aaron Y. Zelin: *"A Closer Look at ISIS,"*, Iraq, 2013.

Abdul Hameed Bakier: *"Internet Jihadists React to the Deaths of Al-Qa'ida's Leaders in Iraq"*, Iraq, 2010.

Ajami, Fouad: *The Syrian Rebellion,* Hoover Institution Press Publication, Stanford: Hoover Institution Press, 2012.

Brian Fishman: *"The Islamic State Returns to Fallujah,"* Iraq and Syria, 2014.

Haney, Antoine; Nicholson, Carter M.: *Conflict Zones: Syria and Mali,* Hauppauge: Nova Science, 2013.

Hashemi, Nader; Postel, Danny: *The Syria Dilemma.* Cambridge: The MIT Press, 2013.

Heydemann, Steven; Leenders, Reinoud: *Middle East Authoritarianisms: Governance, Contestation, and Regime Resilience in Syria and Iran,* Stanford: Stanford University Press, 2013.

Hokayem, Emile: *Syria's Uprising and the Fracturing of the Levant.* Abingdon: Routledge, 2013.

Khatib, Line: *Islamic Revivalism in Syria: The Rise and Fall of Ba'thist Secularism,* Routledge Studies in Political Islam, 2011. Abingdon: Routledge.

Lawson, Fred H.: *Global Security Watch: Syria and Iraq.* Santa Barbara: Praeger, 2013.

Lefèvre, Raphaël: *Ashes of Hama: The Muslim Brotherhood in Syria and Iraq.* New York: Oxford University Press, 2013.

Pierret, Thomas: *Religion and State in Syria: The Sunni Ulama from Coup to Revolution.* Cambridge: Cambridge University Press, 2013.

Ziadeh, Radwan: *Power and Policy in Syria: Intelligence Services, Foreign Relations and Democracy in the Modern Middle East.* London: I.B. Tauris, 2013.

Index

❑❑❑